BE STRONG | STAY STRONG

BE STRONG | STAY STRONG

MIKE KEYES SR.

Be Strong! Stay Strong!: Knowing and Practicing the Seven Spiritual Priorities of Life
ISBN: 978-1-939570-00-0
Copyright © 2010 by Mike Keyes Sr.

Third edition, revised and enlarged

© Mike Keyes, 1988, 1992, 2010

Published by

MKMI Publishing

Mike Keyes Ministries International
PO Box 91916
Tucson, AZ 85752
www.mkmi.org

Joshua 1:8-9

8 This Book of the Law shall not depart from your mouth, but you shall meditate in it day and night, that you may observe to do according to all that is written in it. For then you will make your way prosperous, and then you will have good success.

9 Have I not commanded you? Be strong and of good courage; do not be afraid, nor be dismayed, for the LORD your God is with you wherever you go."

1 Chronicles 28:10

10 Consider now, for the LORD has chosen you to build a house for the sanctuary; be strong, and do it."

Contents

CHAPTER ONE

Be consistent with spiritual priorities

There are many examples throughout the Bible of strong men and women of God who had one thing in common: they were consistent with the things of God. They made plenty of mistakes, but because they served God consistently, they never allowed their mistakes to defeat them or even to slow them down. Although they lived in different times, had different personalities, and accomplished different things for God, they all knew the importance of being consistent in their spiritual lives.

As I have sought God for ways to strengthen my own Christian life, He gave me seven "priorities of life," and emphasized the importance of doing all of them every day. I have discovered that doing these seven things consistently will produce a powerfully victorious life in Jesus Christ. If it works for me, it will work for you, because God is no respecter of persons (see Acts 10:34).

The seven priorities of life

Here is the list of spiritual priorities given to me by the Lord, which I have labored to apply in my life on a daily basis. I can tell you by experience, if you consistently perform these seven things daily, you will grow mighty in God. Guaranteed.

1. Worship
2. Praise
3. Prayer

4. Confession
5. Meditation
6. Study and Reading
7. Sharing

When the Lord gave this list to me, He revealed to me that the list was given in the order of importance. All seven priorities of life are vitally important to our spiritual strength, but in comparison to one another, this list is given in descending order of importance.

In order to stay strong in your spirit, you must perform these seven priorities of life every day. To develop consistency, you don't perform these seven priorities once a week, or every so often, or even when you feel like it, but every day. Consistent Christians are self-motivated. They do these seven priorities every day because they know they need the strength that only consistency will produce.

Their circumstances will have no bearing on their decision to be consistent with these seven priorities of life. In good times or in bad times, the consistent Christian is faithful to perform these seven priorities daily.

Proverbs 6:6–8

6 Go to the ant, you sluggard!
Consider her ways and be wise,

7 Which, having no captain,
Overseer or ruler,

8 Provides her supplies in the summer,
And gathers her food in the harvest.

To develop a track record of consistency, you need to perform all seven priorities daily—not just one or two or three, and not just once in a while. This takes intense discipline, but like the ant in Proverbs 6, the rewards will more than pay off. When winter comes, the ant is sitting pretty because he got out there and worked when no one told him to. In the same way, when you've been hit with one of the devil's surprise attacks, making yourself perform these priorities daily will be something you're thankful to God you did. Doing all seven priorities on a consistent basis will build your spirit in every area and eliminate any weak spots you may have in your spiritual armor. Performing all seven priorities of life every day will produce strength, and strength will produce victory over the devil, his world system, and our flesh.

Spiritual training required

Developing spiritual strength is a process that demands discipline, determination, diligence, and consistency—much like athletic training. In 1 Corinthians 9:26, 27, Paul says, *"Therefore, I run thus: not with uncertainty. Thus I fight: not as one who beats the air. But I discipline my body and bring it into subjection, lest, when I have preached to others, I myself should become disqualified."* In verse 27, Paul describes himself as one who does not beat the air. He uses the sport of boxing to illustrate the principles of spiritual growth and training.

Where do two boxers go after they sign a contract to fight? They head straight to the gym, to begin training for that fight. Each man must train hard every day because he knows his opponent is training hard every day also. Training is not easy. Each boxer must condition himself properly. He must be able to withstand the blows of his opponent. He must have the stamina to go the distance, if necessary, to win. He cannot afford to become tired halfway through the fight. Nor can he afford to underestimate the strength or the abilities of his opponent.

Boxers will train hard for weeks and maybe even months to get ready for a fight that will last no longer than forty-five minutes. Fifteen rounds at three minutes per round totals forty-five minutes of fighting—and many fights don't even go the distance. Yet the two boxers involved will train hundreds of hours for those few minutes in the ring.

The boxer knows that consistency is a must if he expects to win when he steps in the ring on fight night. It takes inner discipline to train consistently for a fight. It's not easy to get up every day and go jogging at 4:00 a.m. It's not easy to lift weights until you're so exhausted you can't lift anymore—every day. It's not easy to exercise and work out every day with sparring partners. It's not easy to discipline your eating habits every day, especially when everyone around you is stuffing themselves like pigs. It's not easy—but the boxer knows there is a price to be paid for victory. He knows victory is not for free. He knows that you must earn your right to be called "Champion." The boxer's body may want to quit many times, but he stays at it because he knows that the big fight is out there ahead of him. He knows he will one day face his opponent in the ring, and if he expects to win, he must be ready. Training is neither exciting nor glamorous. It's hard, monotonous work. Often it is lonely, too. Thousands will pay big bucks for tickets to the fight, and millions more will pay premium prices for pay-for-view to watch the fight live on TV. But how many of them will ever be found down at the gym, watching the training take place? Rarely will you find anyone watching the boxer train as he prepares for the fight. For the most part, people don't care about that part of the process. They just want to see the fight! Well, that's all well and good for the spectators, but for the boxer, he knows better. Despite the emotional and physical loneliness of training, the boxer presses on. Where are the television cameras down at the training facility? Where are all the people who will come to the fight? At the training site? Hardly. The world doesn't care about training bouts—it's the fight that draws the big crowds.

The attention, glamour, praise, excitement and joy come after the fight is won. But without the self-motivation and consistency involved in training, the spoils of victory will never come. If a boxer has not been consistent during training, what will happen when he faces an opponent who has? While the whole world watches, he will be made to look like a fool.

Only the champion is called "great." The crowd applauds his hard work, punching power, and ability to take punishment from his opponent. They talk about how good he is at what he does. They discuss his raw natural talent as a boxer. But how did the champion become champion? Did he just show up one day, proclaim himself champ, and that was it? Did he just cruise down to the gym once or twice a week, for a light workout or two? Did he lift a few weights only when he felt inspired? Did he run a couple of laps every so often? No! A thousand times—no!

The champion became champion because he consistently applied himself seven days a week. He trained hard to develop the strength it took to become champion. He took time to study film on his opponent's moves. He found out what his opponent's strong points were, and located his weak points. He studied the tactics of his opponents as exhibited in previous fights. If they had common opponents in past fights, those fights were reviewed to search for any clues which might be used in preparation and training to gain advantage. Then he developed a strategy. Finally, he worked hard to develop the strength and stamina to put everything he had learned into play. Victory came—but not without a lot of hard work. Natural ability wasn't enough, and it never is. The champion had to be consistent with his training in order to win.

So it is with you and me in our spiritual fights of faith.

Know your adversary

Just as a boxer studies his opponent to learn his every move, we must do the same if we're to prevail in spiritual combat.

1 Peter 5:8–9

8 Be sober, be vigilant; because your adversary the devil walks about like a roaring lion, seeking whom he may devour.

9 Resist him, steadfast in the faith, knowing that the same sufferings are experienced by your brotherhood in the world.

Our adversary is the devil, first and foremost. He is our opponent in this life, and you must understand the fact that he is totally committed to your death and destruction and eternal damnation. He offers no mercy because he doesn't have any. He'll kill you in a heartbeat if you let him. *So don't let him!* Spiritually speaking, when you step into the ring, you're going to need strength to beat the devil. He's very strong and has had a six-thousand-year head start on you, so don't underestimate him for a moment.

Performing the seven priorities of life may seem dull at times, even monotonous—especially since most of these priorities are performed in private. No one sees you as you work on these seven priorities, except the last one. It's just between you and God. That is why you must be as self-motivated as the boxer in training. Your body will not want to perform these seven priorities. Many times you will have to make yourself perform these things. You will have to push yourself like the boxer must push himself to train. These will not be very glamorous or exciting times, because your flesh will fight you every step of the way, but when you step into the ring against the devil, you will find that you have the strength you need, when you need it.

There are many Christians who worship God occasionally, but training occasionally does not get the job done. Some Christians praise the Lord only when they feel like it, but training cannot be based on feelings or the mood of the moment. How many Christians pray consistently? Very few. How many confess the Word of God to any meaningful extent daily? Only a handful. How many Christians actively share their faith on a daily basis? Most Christians have never won a single person to Jesus Christ. With a spiritual training program like that, is it any wonder the devil is beating our brains out? Most Christians never make it through the first round against their spiritual opponent. They go down under a withering barrage of spiritual punch combinations for which they were not prepared. They're down for the count, and God has no choice but to throw in the towel to stop the pitiful mismatch.

Thank God for His mercy, which is new every morning (see Lamentations 3:22, 23). If we find ourselves outmatched and overwhelmed by the devil's onslaught, the Lord will pick us up off the canvas. We're not perfect, and we're all learning as we move along life's way. Even if we lose a particular fight of faith, that's not the end. God will bring us back, and we'll go on to fight another day. There will be many more fights ahead of us, so if we diligently apply ourselves and faithfully practice these seven priorities of life, success against our adversary is guaranteed.

You don't train hard by watching cable TV all day long. You don't train hard sitting on the couch hour after hour, watching football games. You don't train hard by living from one meal to the next, stuffing your stomach with food all day long. You don't train hard wasting hundreds of dollars a month on text messaging. You don't train hard by spending hours on the computer, chatting, surfing, browsing and all the rest. What are you going to do when the next attack comes? Show the devil your profile on Facebook or Twitter? Would a true champion train this way? Of course not!

You must train hard every day. You must be consistent every day. Pray every day. Study and read your Bible every day. Share your faith every day. Worship and praise your God every day. Every day, my friend! That's the key. Institute that kind of training program in your life, and you will put yourself in position to not only resist the devil successfully but to turn the tables on him and actually torment him the way he's trying to torment you. That sounds like fun, don't you think?

CHAPTER TWO

Christians are commanded to be strong

Joshua 1:5–9

5 No man shall be able to stand before you all the days of your life; as I was with Moses, so I will be with you. I will not leave you nor forsake you.

6 Be strong and of good courage, for to this people you shall divide as an inheritance the land which I swore to their fathers to give them.

7 Only be strong and very courageous, that you may observe to do according to all the law which Moses My servant commanded you; do not turn from it to the right hand or to the left, that you may prosper wherever you go.

8 This Book of the Law shall not depart from your mouth, but you shall meditate in it day and night, that you may observe to do according to all that is written in it. For then you will make your way prosperous, and then you will have good success.

9 Have I not commanded you? Be strong and of good courage; do not be afraid, nor be dismayed, for the Lord your God is with you wherever you go.

As Christians, God commands us to be strong. In verse 6, He says, "*Be strong and of a good courage.*" In verse 7, He repeats Himself: "*Only be strong and very courageous."* Then in verse 9, God says, *"Have I not commanded you?"* What is the command? *"To be strong and very courageous."*

God is speaking this same message to us today, just as He did to Joshua many generations ago. These are truths and principles that transcend all generations, so they're for you and me as much as for anyone who has come before us. In fact, I would say that the need for strength has not only remained constant, it has increased proportionately to the rise of sin, perversion, compromise, deception, and false doctrines that have arisen in the last two generations. To be strong and courageous is still a command from God. As Christians we need to take that command seriously if we expect to be pleasing to God.

Throughout the Bible there are verses like these, emphasizing the need to be strong. God's strength is not just for one person or one generation—it is for everybody. Because God is no respecter of persons (see Acts 10:34), if He commands one man to be strong, such as Joshua, He's going to apply that command to all of us—everybody. If He tells one man to be strong, He expects everyone else to be strong also. One person is not responsible for being strong while everyone else gets a free ride. God expects each one of us to understand the command and heed it. Period. In God's army, there is no place for spiritual weaklings.

In John 14:15, Jesus says, *"If you love Me, keep My commandments."* Now, how straightforward is that? It's too simple of a statement to be misunderstood. If we say we love Jesus, we prove that love by knowing and keeping His commandments. If we say we love Jesus but don't keep His commandments, we've become what James calls self-deceived—we've deceived our own heart.

James 1:22

22 But be doers of the word, and not hearers only, deceiving yourselves.

Don't be self-deceived.

Many Christians do not realize that God commands them to be strong. Joshua 1:9 is a command. It is not an exhortation. It is not a request. It is not something God would like us to be if we feel like it or one day get around to it. No, He commands us to be strong today and every day we live on this earth.

Again, many Christians say they love Jesus, but they're not keeping this commandment to be strong in the Lord and in the power of His might (see Ephesians 6:10). In my opinion, after reading God's Word and serving Him full time in ministry since 1978, I'm convinced God is not at all pleased with weak Christians. I believe He puts up with their weakness, but I don't believe He likes it one bit. I don't believe God is pleased with weak churches, pastored by weak pastors and filled with weak people. He may put up with it, but He doesn't like it. God commands us to be strong, so He's commanding you to be strong.

1 Chronicles 28:10

10 Consider now, for the Lord has chosen you to build a house for the sanctuary; be strong, and do it.

No excuses accepted! Jesus has given us an assignment—a commandment to go into all the world and preach His gospel. We're called and commissioned to be a co-worker with God in building His "house," which is the worldwide body of Christ. In the times of David and Solomon, which is the timeframe for our verse from 1 Chronicles, David was talking to Solomon about building an actual building—the temple of the Lord. But in our case today, although the truth of that verse still applies, God's not talking about building a physical structure of some kind. He's talking about having the strength to fulfill the Great Commission (see Mark 16:15–18, Matthew 28:18–20). The "house" we're commanded to build is a spiritual house, not a physical house. To do that, we need to be strong.

What is strength?

Since God commands us to be strong, we need to know what strength is— not according to what men think, but what God thinks. Since He's the one commanding us to be strong, we'll stand judgment for this according to His definition of strength, not some man's somewhere.

What is God's definition for strength? Nehemiah 8:10 says, "*The joy of the Lord is your strength.*" But there's more. Not only is God's joy a definition for spiritual strength, but the Lord showed me there is another definition for spiritual strength.

In the 1980s, I used to do a lot of jogging as a way for me to try to stay physically fit. (I don't jog anymore as it was damaging my knees, hips, and ankles. Now instead, I've taken up bicycling, which is much easier on one's joints.) But back then, I would go jogging three or four times a week in the heat of the day—to make it as hard as I could on myself. I wanted to jog at the hottest time of the day so it would be as punishing as possible. My objective was to be as strong as I could be physically for the Lord's work, and to do that, I felt I needed to do the jogging in the early afternoon, rather than early in the morning.

One day while jogging along, I began to think about strength, and how God defines it. I had been praying and seeking God along these lines in my study and prayer times. I was using my jogging as an opportunity to get quiet in spirit and listen. As I jogged along, the Holy Spirit suddenly spoke up in my heart and said, *I will give you another definition for spiritual strength.* He then said, *Strength can also be defined as consistency of action.* I had never heard anyone define strength like that before, so when I finished my jog and went home, I immediately wrote that phrase down on a piece of paper. Later, after I got cleaned up, I went into my office and began to study God's Word to see if that statement lined up with Scripture. As I studied from both the Old Testament and New, I found that this definition was in complete agreement with what the Scriptures had to say.

Consistency of our actions is spiritual strength_____

Consistency of action will produce strength in our lives—there is no doubt about it. I believe spiritual weakness is a product of spiritual inconsistency. If you look around, you can plainly see that if Christians are consistent about anything, it's their inconsistency! In order to be strong and then stay strong, there are certain things we must do every day. The Christian who is consistent with the things of God never allows his surrounding circumstances to govern him. The world is full of fear, now more than ever before. It's also full of uncertainty and global turmoil. The consistent Christian will walk above all of this confusion. In good times or bad times, the consistent Christian stays consistent—he or she stays at it. Consistent Christians know the promises of God never change, so if they continue doing their spiritual priorities faithfully each day, God will take care of them because He has already told us He exalts His Word above His own Name.

Psalms 138:2–3

2 … For You have magnified Your word above all Your name.

3 In the day when I cried out, You answered me,
And made me bold with strength in my soul.

Notice that God puts His Word above His own Name, so that when we cry out for answers, He is quick to answer! As we stand on His promises, He delights in upholding His Word to us in whatever ways we need His help. According to Jeremiah 1:12, He actually watches over His Word to perform it, which means He guards His Word and always makes sure it comes to pass for anyone with faith and strength enough to believe it. That's why, according to verse 3, He can make such consistent people *"bold with strength from our soul."* This is why the consistent Christian always wins out in the end. He outlasts the devil, the world system, and the dead-to-sin flesh. No matter how long it takes for victory to manifest, he has the inner strength to persevere and prevail until the unseen becomes the seen.

Keep going despite your mistakes and failures

When a consistent believer makes a mistake, he is quick to ask God for forgiveness. Once he asks for it, he believes he receives that forgiveness by faith, not feelings. With God's forgiveness accepted and received, the consistent believer moves on, taking his cue from the Apostle Paul himself.

Philippians 3:12–16

12 Not that I have already attained, or am already perfected; but I press on, that I may lay hold of that for which Christ Jesus has also laid hold of me.

13 Brethren, I do not count myself to have apprehended; but one thing I do, forgetting those things which are behind and reaching forward to those things which are ahead,

14 I press toward the goal for the prize of the upward call of God in Christ Jesus.

15 Therefore let us, as many as are mature, have this mind; and if in anything you think otherwise, God will reveal even this to you.

16 Nevertheless, to the degree that we have already attained, let us walk by the same rule, let us be of the same mind.

Just like everybody else, Paul had skeletons in his closet. He had a past that wasn't right in God's eyes, and he knew it. But Paul also had a revelation about the power and gift of God's mercy and forgiveness and learned to walk in the light of it all the days of his ministry life. The "one thing" he did on a consistent basis was to forget the mistakes and sins of the past and reach forward to the future, pressing towards the goal of one day hearing Jesus say to him, "*Well done, good and faithful servant.*" In other words, as a consistent Christian, he learned how to move on from his sins, failures, and mistakes. He didn't let the devil condemn him over the past—he walked in the light of God's mercy and forgiveness and moved on.

This is why, as an example, he could write to the Corinthians and say this to them:

2 Corinthians 7:2

2 Open your hearts to us. We have wronged no one, we have corrupted no one, we have cheated no one.

Wait a minute! Is this man telling the truth to the Corinthians, or not? Isn't he the man over in Acts chapters 8 and 9, who not only held the coats of those who stoned Stephen to death, but was happy they did it? Isn't this the guy who "breathed out slaughter" against the disciples of the Lord, arrested them, and threw them in prison? Isn't he the one who was on his way to Damascus to arrest more Christians when he had his encounter with Jesus? Yes, it's the same man—or is it?

Physically, it's the same guy. Spiritually, he's different. He's been born again. Old things passed away, and all things became new. His sins, which were many, were all washed away and forgiven by the blood of Jesus, and now he's a new creature in Christ, walking in the light of his forgiveness every day.

Go back and read that passage from Philippians carefully. Don't just stop after verse 14. Read and meditate on verses 15 and 16, because they're an important part of this truth being revealed by the Holy Spirit. Not only did Paul forget the past that concerned his activities before he got saved on the road to Damascus, but he had learned to walk by the same rule every day after that. In other words, he learned that mature believers think and walk this way on a daily basis. They don't allow the devil to hold their sins and past failures over their heads forever. They receive forgiveness for sins committed today, in exactly the same way they received forgiveness for the sins committed prior to accepting Jesus as Lord and Savior. This is a great truth many Christians never learn or apply, but consistent Christians have done both.

Also notice that God expects His children to walk and live this way. In verse 15, God says that if anyone thinks otherwise, He will reveal this to them. That means He doesn't want us living in the past. He wants us to trust His mercy and promise to forgive, no matter how we feel about it. God wants us to "have this mind," walking in the constant mercy and forgiveness of God, and moving on from sin, failure, and past mistakes, just like Paul did. God will "reveal" this to us, and let us know He doesn't want us allowing the devil to beat us over the heads for sins that have already been confessed and forgiven.

Fall forward

The consistent Christian has learned from his mistakes, and doesn't allow those failures to condemn him or drag him down. In other words, when he falls, he falls forward, never backwards. The Christian who falls forward will still be moving forward as he falls. When he gets up again, he will still be two steps ahead of where he was when he fell. By falling forward, the consistent Christian will still be on the advance—even if he should stumble into sin. On the other hand, the man who falls backward will lose ground spiritually because of his sins. He will regress rather than progress. Through a lack of consistency with the seven priorities of life, he will be an easy target for the enemy, and allow his failures to impede his progress with God in life and ministry.

All of us make mistakes at one time or another, but if we are consistent, we will never allow those sins to stop our growth in the Lord. We'll be quick to repent and get those sins under the blood of Jesus. Even though a consistent Christian may fall, he keeps going forward. Day in and day out he is the same. This, then, is the mark of a consistent Christian.

Strength is not the possession of power or ability. It's more than having or possessing the joy of the Lord. The Holy Spirit is the power and ability of God in our hearts and lives, yet I have observed that many who have the Holy Spirit are still weak in their spirits. Possessing the power and ability of God is not enough to make us and keep us strong. You need consistency with the seven priorities of life. In the same way, people can experience and enjoy the joy of their salvation at certain times along life's way, but I've seen very few who can hold onto that joy consistently.

The truth is that all Christians have the potential to be strong because the Holy Spirit lives in their hearts, and all Christians can let the joy of the Lord be their strength whenever necessary. But until you develop the habit of spiritual consistency with the seven priorities of life, these great gifts from God will continue to lie dormant within us. Our potential for greatness in Christ must be developed, the same way a boxer's talents must be developed before he can earn the right to be called the champion. The only way a Christian can do this is through consistency of action—by taking care of the seven spiritual priorities daily.

The consistent man does not draw a lot of attention to himself. He quietly stays at it until the battle is won. The consistent believer is the one who beats the devil because he has developed the strength necessary to do the job. The devil doesn't leave because we love the Lord—he leaves because he's thrown out. After all, what do the words "cast out" mean anyway? We talk frequently about casting out demons and devils out of people, or out of their finances, or out of their marriages, etc. Well, to "cast" means to "throw." So, to cast out is to throw out. The devil isn't going anywhere in your life, honey, until you get up the strength to throw him out of your house, off your porch, and out of your life. Many Christians have not learned this yet. They think that if they shout real loud in church, the devil will leave them alone. They think that if they attend all the conferences, camp meetings, and revivals, the devil will leave them alone. They think that if they buy up all the speaker's books and CDs, the devil will leave them alone. It's not happening, baby! He will leave you alone when you so torment him that he wants to leave you alone!

Yes, we need to attend the revivals, church services, conferences, and camp meetings. By all means, buy as much of good faith-building material as you can. Feed on good teaching whenever possible. But all of those things alone will not keep the devil off your back. Many Christians jump, shout, dance, run, and swing from the lights, yet they still live lives of spiritual inconsistency and therefore spiritual defeat.

We need to sing and be free in the Lord, but we must also realize that it is consistency concerning all the things of God that will make us victorious Christians. I have discovered through my experience that consistency of action wears the devil down and ultimately brings victory. It may take awhile, but if you're committed to excellence and consistency in Christ, time isn't a factor. You'll become the doer of Ephesians 6:13, which says:

Ephesians 6:13

13 Therefore take up the whole armor of God, that you may be able to withstand in the evil day, and having done all, to stand.

What does it mean when the Bible tells us that having done all, we're to stand? Other translations say that when we've done everything, we're to stand. In other words, we do everything we're commanded to do by God, and then we stand our ground for as long as it takes before victory is won.

Whenever I attend one of those big Christian conventions or camp meetings, I wonder where all the people go once the meeting is over. During those services, we clap our hands, stomp our feet, lift our hands to heaven, run around the building, have a march outside in the parking lot, and in general are very demonstrative in our worship and praise to the Lord. Yes, we're quite bold while attending the convention, but are we that bold when facing the enemy on the field of battle? It's easy to sing and shout when we're surrounded by thousands of others who are all doing the same thing. But let's see how well we sing and shout when we're standing all alone against the enemies of our soul. Can you still shout "victory" without the support of the crowd? Many Christians cannot.

It's easy to quote scriptures down at the church, but can we successfully apply the Word effectively when we're under attack? Facing the congregation to declare what we believe is one thing, but facing the devil's lies, sickness or disease, unpaid bills, lay-offs and job terminations, unsaved relatives, and rebellious children or spouses is something else entirely. It's easy to praise the Lord when we've got an anointed choir, a gifted song leader, and a polished preacher down at the church. But what happens in the car after church, when we've gone home? The devil doesn't attack us at the church—he attacks us where we live. Therefore, that's where consistency is needed the most.

We quote Romans 8:37, declaring ourselves to be "more than conquerors," but then wilt under fire when we see the chaos and turmoil all around us. There's nothing like coming home from work and finding your kids high on dope or one of your visiting relatives drunk in the corner with an empty bottle of Jack Daniels. A lot of us are more or less prepared for some anticipated kind of attack, but what about the surprise attacks? What happens when the devil blindsides you with something from totally out in the blue? Spiritual strength is not needed down at the convention center or at the Bible study. It's needed at home, on the job, in the streets, on the airplanes, or wherever the devil comes against you. When the devil launches his next surprise attack against you, are you ready for it? Are you prepared? Whether you're expecting the unexpected or not, you must have the strength to walk in victory seven days a week, fifty-two weeks a year. That kind of strength only comes through consistency with the things of God—those seven priorities of life.

In this day and hour, Christians need to be strong or they will find themselves in big trouble. Satan knows he has but a short time, so he is doing all he can to defeat Christians while he still has the opportunity. If believers are not strong and courageous in the things of God, the devil will have us for lunch. God's command to be strong and courageous isn't for His benefit, but for ours. We are the ones who need to be strong because we are the ones who must face and defeat the enemy.

CHAPTER THREE

Be strong and stay strong

1 Corinthians 16:13–14

13 Watch, stand fast in the faith, be brave, be strong.

14 Let all that you do be done with love.

In the King James Version of the Bible, verse 13 is translated like this, *"Watch ye, stand fast in the faith, quit you like men, be strong."* I like the part of that rendering that says we're to "quit [conduct ourselves] like men and be strong." That simply means we're to act like a man, like who we already are in Christ. Romans 8:37 tells us we're more than conquerors in Christ. In this verse, Paul reminds the Corinthians to act like who Christ has made them to be.

Here is how the New American Standard Bible translation renders this verse passage: *"Be on the alert, stand firm in the faith, act like men, be strong."* Other more modern translations give similar renderings—all with the same emphasis. God wants us to act like men and be strong. Period. According to 1 Chronicles 28:10, He expects us to be strong enough to do anything and everything required of us as soldiers in the army of the Lord. No excuses can be given for failure, because none will be accepted.

In order to act like a man in God's sight, we must be consistent to become strong in spirit. This applies to both men and women, because our spirits are neither male or female in a sexual context. Galatians 3:28 says it this way: *"There is neither Jew nor Greek, there is neither bond or free, there is neither male nor female; for you are one in Christ Jesus."* Therefore, "masculine" in the spiritual sense of the word is different than "masculine" in the physical sense of the word. In the natural realm, our five physical sense world in which we live now, masculinity is always connected with men—not women. In the same way femininity is always connected with women—not men.

But in the spirit world it's different. Spirits are masculine without gender. God is a "He," not a "She," yet He, along with all other spirits we know about—angels, demons, etc.—are gender free because the sexes are part of God's plan for how we are to procreate on earth—a wonderful way to enjoy reproduction when done God's way and not man's way.

But when it comes to the world's twisted ideas of what a "man" is supposed to be, you need to remember it's always based upon the flesh, never the spirit. God's idea of a man is spirit-based. The world's idea of a man is body-based. Over the years, I'm sure you can recall vivid advertising images about the world's idea of manhood. Remember the commercials for Marlboro cigarettes? That tobacco company made millions of dollars in sales because they successfully developed and advertised the Marlboro Man. Remember? If you're too young to remember, trust me on this one! For years, the Marlboro Man was plastered all over town on billboards, in magazines, and on TV, before cigarette advertising was banned on TV. The image was clear and the message unmistakable. If you want to be a real man like the Marlboro Man, put that cancer stick in your mouth, light it up, and there you are. You've become a "man," ready to go rope cattle, sleep in the prairie with rocks under your back, your saddle as the pillow, smelling as bad as the cattle. What a joke! It'd be funny if it weren't so spiritually pathetic. That kind of a "man" is pure foolishness in God's sight.

And by the way, nobody from the advertising world ever takes time to show you the Marlboro Man years later, when he's laid up in his hospital bed, wheezing in pain and dying a slow, painful death because of lung cancer. They don't bother showing you that part of the Marlboro Man's life, and they never will. The world's lies always deal with immediate gratification and avoid all mention of how today's pleasures will reap tomorrow's pain, anguish and regret. Hebrews 11:25 says it best. There is pleasure in sin—but *"only for a season."* Moses knew it, and you and I better know it, too.

Be strong in the Lord

Ephesians 6:10

10 Finally, my brethren, be strong in the Lord and in the power of His might.

God wants us to be strong in His might. As Christians, we cannot look for excuses as to why we are not strong, because there aren't any. 1 John 4:4 says, "*Greater is he that is in you, than he that is in the world,*" so that eliminates all of our excuses for failure. And then there's one of my all-time favorites, found in 1 Chronicles 28:10.

1 Chronicles 28:10

10 Consider now, for the Lord has chosen you to build a house for the sanctuary; be strong, and do it.

This command from God leaves no room for misunderstanding. It's too simple, too straightforward, too easy to understand. God is giving us the assignment to go into all the world, preach the gospel, and work with Him to win souls. It doesn't matter what the devil throws up against us. God said be strong enough to repel any and all attacks of the enemy—period. No excuses. No special exemptions. None. You've been told to go build God's sanctuary, so go do it! Don't come back to God whining and complaining about how hard it is, because you're just wasting your time. He won't have any part of it. In Matthew 16:18, Jesus said He will build His church, and the gates of hell will not prevail against it. That pretty much sums it up, don't you think? No matter what the devil may do to try and stop us, it can't succeed. Why? Because Jesus said it couldn't, and if He says so, then it's so. Romans 8:37 says we're more than conquerors through Christ Jesus. So, get off your blessed assurance, and go out there and conquer something in the Name of Jesus. On and on I could go, but you get the point. There are no excuses for failure.

If God tells me to hold an outdoor crusade in some remote village in the Philippines in the middle of the rainy season, I can't say "no" just because it has been raining every day for weeks. Jesus spoke to the wind and the water in Mark 4:39, and He expects me to do the same. Why? Because the same authority in which He operated is the same authority in which I operate. Here's what He said about what we can or can't do in this life in His Name: *"He that believeth on me, the works that I do shall he do also; and greater works than these shall he do"* (see John 14:12 KJV). According to this statement, if the wind and rain stopped when Jesus spoke to the weather while in that boat on the lake, then it will work the same way for me whenever I need for it to. If the weather poses a problem to the crusade that God tells me to conduct, He expects me to do something about that with the authority I've been given in Christ Jesus. He expects me to talk to the clouds, and make them go away in Jesus' Name. "You mean we can do such things, Brother Mike?" Exactly. Absolutely. Without a doubt. I've done it, and you can do it too. God is no respecter of persons (see Acts 10:34).

You don't need to go to somebody's Bible school to get qualified to walk in God's strength and anointing. A diploma or certificate on your wall doesn't make you anything in God's eyes, or the devil's either. It's when we're out there under fire, doing battle in the Name of Jesus—then we find out how valuable we are to God. God expects us to be who Jesus has made us to be, and that means we move mountains whenever they get in our way. Quit waiting around for God to do something, because He's already done everything that needs to be done about the devil on earth. Jesus already stripped him of all power and authority and gave all of that back to us, His church (see Matthew 28:18–20). So, go ahead! Speak to those clouds in Jesus' Name. Don't be afraid to do it. Jesus spoke to wind, rain, waves, dead children, and fig trees, and it didn't seem to bother God one bit. In fact, it glorifies God when we do what He intended all along—to exercise dominion (see Genesis 1:26–28). Of course, if people see you talking to the sky, they'll think you've lost your mind, but be of good cheer beloved—you're in good company. They thought Jesus had lost His mind, too, and He said the servant isn't above His Master. If they persecuted Jesus like this, you can be sure they'll do the very same with you. But that's okay. You're not talking to things to impress people—you're doing it because you're commanded to by God. It's what He expects, so never mind what people think. You won't stand before their judgment seat someday, but God's. Think about that next time you're pressured to clam up just because you're afraid someone might be laughing at you.

On one occasion the Lord told me to hold a seven-day outdoor crusade in Cotabato City, located on the island of Mindanao, in the Philippines.

However, the dates He gave me for this crusade were in the middle of the rainy season. So, what did my staff and I do? We spoke to the weather and commanded all the rain to leave for the duration of the crusade in Jesus' Name. The result? It rained hard every day right up to the day we came to town and started the crusade. In the presence of local cooperating pastors, my crusade team, and anyone else close enough to listen, I rebuked the rain and the clouds and praised the Lord for sunny weather. We prayed, "No more rain in Jesus' Name!" It didn't rain for the next seven days. It was perfect weather each day for the crowds to come and hear the gospel—warm, sunny, and very pleasant. The day after our crusade ended, it poured down rain again—but by that time the damage had been done to the devil's kingdom. Thousands were saved and healed during those seven days, and there was nothing the devil could do to stop it. Not only did God get the glory in this, but it provided a great object lesson for the pastors who participated. They'd never seen anyone talk to the weather like that before, and it was a great way to teach faith, authority, and spiritual strength to men and women of God who needed to know.

The rainy season is no excuse for waiting. If God tells you to go somewhere for a rainy-season crusade, you can be sure there's a reason why, and it has to do with saving souls. Waiting could be spiritually fatal for untold multitudes, and I'm not going to take the chance of having their blood on my hands someday when I am judged for the life I've lived (see Ezekiel 3 and 33). If I'm waiting around for dry season instead of being in the right place at the right time with the right message, how many may die lost or move out of town while we wait for dry weather? As Christians, we must realize that our spiritual strength may make the difference between someone going to heaven instead of hell. There can be no truth as sobering as that.

In and of ourselves, we are no match for the devil, his world system, the natural forces of this planet, and our own dead flesh. But in Christ, everything changes. The great exchange takes place, and as we wait upon the Lord, His strength becomes ours.

Isaiah 40:28–31

28 Have you not known?
   Have you not heard?

The everlasting God, the Lord,
The Creator of the ends of the earth,
Neither faints nor is weary.
His understanding is unsearchable.

29 He gives power to the weak,
And to those who have no might He increases strength.

30 Even the youths shall faint and be weary,
And the young men shall utterly fall,

31 But those who wait on the Lord
Shall renew their strength;
They shall mount up with wings like eagles,
They shall run and not be weary,
They shall walk and not faint.

Remember Ephesians 6:10? We're told to be strong in the Lord, and in the power of His might. How is that done? By doing what these verses here tell us to. Waiting upon God creates what I call "The Great Exchange." The word "renew" in verse 31 can also be rendered "exchange." We could then say it this way: *those who wait upon the Lord shall exchange their strength.* What is exchanged? Strength. We give God our strength, which is pitifully woeful, and we get in exchange His strength, which is more than a match for any enemy we'll ever face in this life, times ten. All things are possible when we learn to exchange our strength for God's. We must always remember that Jesus gave all of His authority to those in His body still on earth, which includes you if you're sitting there reading this book. We are that body of Christ on earth today, and God can only do what the body does because He lives in us.

People wonder all the time why God doesn't seem to get involved the way they think He should, when it's never a matter of God getting involved, but rather, a matter of His body getting involved. Does God do things on His own from time to time? It might seem that way, because we can't see things from His divine perspective. But because all authority has been delegated to the church by Jesus, it's really up to us to exercise that authority and get in the game in the Name of Jesus. I know that runs cross-grain to what many believers teach and believe, but it's all through the Bible and beyond debate as far as I'm concerned. When things happen and we all marvel at what God seemed to do arbitrarily, you can be sure someone somewhere was praying and taking dominion in the Name of Jesus. You may never know who, what, where, and when in terms of who was using their delegated authority, but rest assured, when the rewards are passed out someday in heaven, we'll all get to see who the unsung heroes of faith, authority, and spiritual strength really were.

Yes, 1 Corinthians 12 talks about the gifts of the Spirit operating as the Spirit wills, but we're not talking about those gifts here. We're talking about using our authority to get a job done for God. In that respect, as I said, God isn't going to do one thing more about the devil. It's up to us, His body of Christ on earth, to take the gift of delegated authority, and exercise it in Jesus' Name. Period.

Therefore, if you don't preach, Jesus can't preach. If you don't lay hands on the sick, Jesus can't lay hands on the sick. Why? It's simple. Jesus is the Head, but we're His body, and the Head can only do what the body does. Think about that. Physically speaking, your head is attached to your neck, which is attached to the rest of you. You think and make decisions up in your head, but how are those decisions carried out? Through the body. You can decide to walk into the next room and get a cup of coffee, but guess what? If your body doesn't take your head there, you're not going to get your cuppa joe. In the same way, Jesus needs His body to understand their importance to His plans and purposes on earth. We must be strong because Jesus needs a strong body through which to manifest Himself. A strong head is useless without a strong body. If you doubt that, take a day and go visit a hospital or convalescent home. Look at the many people in places like that who have active minds, but sick, injured or withering bodies. They want to get up and go live life like normal people, but that old, sick, or injured body won't let them.

A startling vision revelation

Brother Kenneth E. Hagin was my spiritual grandfather. More than any other man, Brother Hagin was responsible for rooting me and grounding me in the truth of faith, authority, and many other topics that through the years have enabled me to stand strong against any and all enemy attacks. In his book *I Believe in Visions*, Brother Hagin talks at length about some of the visions he was given during the time of his ministry on earth. In one of those visions, Jesus was talking with Brother Hagin when all of a sudden, an evil spirit came up and tried to disrupt the meeting. Here is the excerpt from Brother Hagin's book in his own words:

> While Jesus was talking to me, an evil spirit that looked like a monkey ran between Jesus and me and spread out something that looked like a black cloud or a smoke screen. I couldn't see Jesus anymore.
>
> Then the demon began jumping up and down, waving his arms and legs, and yelling in a shrill voice, "yakety-yak, yakety-yak, yakety-yak."
>
> I paused for a moment. I could hear the voice of Jesus as He continued to talk to me, but I could not understand the words He was saying.
>
> I thought to myself, *Doesn't the Lord know I am missing what He is saying? I need to get that—it's important—but I am missing it.* I wondered why Jesus didn't command the evil spirit to stop talking. I waited for a few more moments. Jesus continued talking as if He didn't even know the evil spirit were present. I wondered why the Lord didn't cast him out, but He didn't.
>
> Finally, in desperation, I pointed my finger at the evil spirit and said, "I command you to be quiet in the Name of Jesus Christ!" He stopped immediately and fell to the floor. The black smokescreen disappeared and I could see Jesus once again. The spirit lay on the floor whimpering and whining like a whipped pup. I said, "Not only must you be quiet, but get up and get out of here!" He got up and ran away.
>
> I was still wondering why Jesus had not stopped this evil spirit from interfering, and of course Jesus knew what I was thinking. He said, "If you hadn't done something about that, I couldn't have."
>
> "Lord, I know I misunderstood You! You said You *couldn't* do anything about it, but You really meant that You *wouldn't*."
>
> "No," He said, "if you hadn't done something about that spirit, I couldn't have."
>
> "But, Lord, you can do *anything*. To say You couldn't is different from anything I've ever heard preached or preached myself. This really upends my theology."

"Sometimes your theology needs upending," the Lord answered.

I said, "I have read through the New Testament 150 times and many portions of it more than that. If that is in there, I don't know about it."

"Son, there is a lot in there you don't know," the Lord pointed out. "There is not a single place in the New Testament where believers are ever told to pray against the devil and I will do anything about him. There is not one instance in any of the epistles written to the churches that said to tell God to rebuke the devil or do something about the devil. To pray that God the Father or I the Lord Jesus Christ will rebuke the devil or do anything about the devil, is a waste of time. God has done all He is going to do about the devil for the time being until the angel comes down from heaven, takes the chain and binds him, and puts him into the bottomless pit.

"Every writer of the New Testament in writing to the Church always told *the believer* to do something about the devil. The believer has to have authority over the devil, or the Bible wouldn't tell him to do something about the devil:

Matthew 28:18–20

18 And Jesus came and spoke to them, saying, "All authority has been given to Me in heaven and on earth.

19 Go therefore and make disciples of all the nations, baptizing them in the name of the Father and of the Son and of the Holy Spirit,

20 teaching them to observe all things that I have commanded you; and lo, I am with you always, even to the end of the age." Amen.

"You might say, 'But you could have done something about that evil spirit because this Scripture says you have all power and authority in heaven and in earth.' However, I have delegated my authority on the earth to the Church.

Mark 16:15–18

15 And He said to them, "Go into all the world and preach the gospel to every creature.

16 He who believes and is baptized will be saved; but he who does not believe will be condemned.

17 And these signs will follow those who believe: In My name they will cast out demons; they will speak with new tongues;

18 they will take up serpents; and if they drink anything deadly, it will by no means hurt them; they will lay hands on the sick, and they will recover."

"One of the first signs mentioned that will follow believers is that they should cast out devils. That means that in My Name they will exercise authority over the devil. I delegated My authority over the devil to the Church, and I can work only *through* the Church, for I am the Head of the Church.

"In writing to believers, James said, ' ...Resist the devil, and he will flee from you' (see James 4:7). James didn't say to get God to resist the devil for you. He said, 'You resist the devil and he will flee from you.'"

(I Believe in Visions, pp 77–80)

Proverbs 19:27

27 Cease listening to instruction, my son,
And you will stray from the words of knowledge.

That vision wasn't just for Brother Hagin. It is for all of us in the body of Christ, which is His Church. We all need to know, and if necessary, be reminded, about the fact that in Christ, we have all the strength and authority to torment the devil at every turn. This was one of the greatest revelations God gave me in the early days of my walk with God, and I thank Him for it. Only God knows how I would have struggled if I hadn't known these truths.

When I first came to the Philippines in September, 1980, I found in a very short time that I was not nearly as strong in spirit as I thought I was. Not only was I all alone, but there were no more great churches to be a member of or great sermons or church services off of which to feed. No more

Christian bookstores on every corner. No more "Message-of-the-Month" club to join. In those early days, there was no Internet, no streaming video, no cell phones with international calling capability. No text messaging, no instant messaging, no chatting, no CDs. Fax machines didn't even begin showing up until the late 1980s, and even then, they never worked half the time because the phone lines were so bad. It would be an all-day project just to get one or two pages faxed through successfully to the U.S.

No, for the first fifteen years or so, it was just me and my Bible. My spiritual father, Rev. Buddy Harrison, lived in Tulsa, Oklahoma, U.S. We saw each other once every few years, and then it was only for a brief few days or so. No more attending big, anointed Christian seminars, camp meetings, conferences or conventions. In the Philippines, in those days, a large church was a church of fifty people. In the interior jungles and mountains, the church attendance was even smaller. Many times we had more animals in the church than people. Many times we were so high up along the mountain ridges, that clouds would be rolling through the church during the messages. Half the people would disappear as I was preaching, but I knew they were still there because I could hear them saying "amen" to my message points!

No nice hotels to sleep in. No resorts to visit to "come away" and be refreshed. No vacations. No private vehicles either. Wherever we went, we took public transportation, which if you've ever been to the Philippines, you know how bad it is. But there's more. Sleeping on the roof of ships on their overnight voyages from island to island because they were already overloaded below deck. Hanging on the sides of buses for hours because there were no more buses, and this was the last one out of town. Stuffed into Jeepneys (the Filipino version of a public taxi) and little, skinny pan boats, with goats, pigs, chickens, sacks of rice, surrounded and pressed upon by people who probably hadn't bathed in weeks. Temperatures above 100 degrees, and no air conditioning in any of these vehicles or boats.

When we got off or got out, we started walking. We walked, and walked, and walked, and walked. Some days we walked, hiked and climbed 26 or 27 miles, just to reach a church of three or four people. No "armor bearer" to carry my Bible or my backpack. Are you kidding? Sometimes we were so far up or into the mountains, some of these people hadn't ever even seen a white man before, much less know enough to offer to help me carry my things. There was no nice bed to sleep on after service. Imagine trying to sleep in 100% humidity, no breath of wind whatsoever, no air conditioning, and hundreds of mosquitoes buzzing you all night long. Waking up covered in mosquito bites, or soaked in your own bloody clothes because you slept on a bed infested with bed bugs who sucked your blood all night long. If I even had a bed, it was a wooden slab, no mattress of any kind. Many times we slept on the floor, and many times that floor was dirt. No pillow or blankets. Many nights my Bible was my pillow, and we shivered through until morning. During rainy season, we did this kind of walking and hiking in pouring, driving rain storms, preaching in soaking wet clothes, and no dry clothes to put on since your backpack was soaked through as well. Sleeping in soaking wet clothes, with wind whipping through the little huts we stayed in, to get up next day and do it all over again—day after day for weeks.

I quickly discovered that I had only been cruising on someone else's revelation of spiritual strength. It certainly wasn't mine, that's for sure. I realized I had been riding on someone else's back when it came to faith and spiritual strength. It was during those times that I realized that I couldn't play "gospel games" anymore. When the Lord tells you to go into the mountains and preach, you have to have the strength to do it—without murmuring, grumbling, or complaining all the way.

That means you have to be consistent in performing your seven priorities each day.

Proverbs 3:1–2

1 My son, do not forget my law,
   But let your heart keep my commands;

2 For length of days and long life
   And peace they will add to you.

Remember, we're commanded to be strong, and because strength is defined as consistency of action, we're commanded to be consistent. This will produce the level of strength necessary to have a long, peaceful, productive, and satisfying life.

Be strong—or else!

I am an apostle to the Philippines. That is my area of calling, and I must understand the challenges that come with the territory. The Filipino people are beautiful in so many ways, and the country is one of the most breathtaking countries on earth in terms of natural beauty and scenery. But on the other side of that coin, the Philippines is also a rugged country, and for a long time, it's been a country beset with civil war and terrorism. If you are not strong in a country like this, one of two things will happen to you. One, you will be completely ineffective for God, and eventually go home utterly defeated and discouraged. Or two, you'll be sent home in a casket, dead. Over the years since 1980, I've seen some very sincere people come to the Philippines with great excitement and spiritual anticipation. But in so many cases, these same people became a curse instead of a blessing because they weren't strong in their spirits. They sincerely desired to be a blessing, but instead became a burden. I have also seen sincere people come to the Philippines to do a work for God, and die on the field.

Is it God's will for such things to happen? Of course not. Problems came because the people were not strong in their spirits. As Christians, we must learn that sincerity does not equate with spiritual strength. In the course of my ministry and calling to the Philippines, I have found that many Christians are sincere, but sincerely weak in spirit at the same time.

You know, when the Lord tells me to go up into the mountains and preach, I have to be strong enough to do it. Remember, there are no excuses for failure or disobedience. He's already told us to be strong to do whatever it is He wants us to do (see 1 Chronicles 28:10), so I'm to blame if I'm not tough enough, strong enough, and determined enough to get to the top of the mountain in the Name of Jesus. That means I have to be consistent in performing those seven priorities every day. Failure to do so could cost me my life, and yours, too, if you're along for the ride. Nine or ten weeks in the mountains and jungles of the Philippines is a long time. There are no doctors up in the mountains. No urgent care facilities. No drugstores. No available transportation to get you down for medical attention either—except your own two feet. If you get sick up there, your faith must produce results because there are no other ways to find relief. Either you will have enough strength to stand, or you will look for the first opportunity to quit and go home.

Mountain ministry is hard on the physical body. It seems that you are always climbing, and many times you must climb in the rain. If you climb during the rainy season, the paths you follow become rivers of mud, and when you get to the church where you are scheduled to minister, you must do so in your soaking wet, muddy clothing. There are no washers or dryers in the mountains, so you wear what you have on for as long as it takes before you find a river or stream where somebody washes your clothes by hand and lets them dry by the heat of the sun. In the dry season, your clothes will become soaked with sweat and your body covered with dust from the pathways. The tropical heat is stifling, and the humidity is almost always near the 100% mark.

You climb and climb, wading through rivers and hiking many miles to reach the next church before dark. When you get there, you can't stop to rest because it's time for service, and the people gathered to hear you preach have already been waiting for hours. You put your bags down, pull out your Bible, and start preaching. There are no microphones or sound systems in the mountain churches, so—even if your throat is sore from preaching non-stop for days on end—you must speak out strongly and assertively if you expect the people to hear and receive from you. On many occasions, because your attendance is such a rare event for so many of the believers up there, they'll have you speak three or four times a day for weeks. Therefore, you must use your faith to keep from losing your voice and falling over from exhaustion.

When it's time for bed, you sleep on a bed with no mattress or cushion whatsoever. Your "bed" is made of wooden boards, and many times, as I've said before, your Bible becomes your pillow because that's all there is. Up in the mountainous areas of the Philippines, many homes don't even have the wooden beds. In that case, you sleep on the floor, which might be of wood or plain old dirt. Having experienced all that I write about here, I can say that if you're not consistent with the seven priorities of life, you'll never make it.

Swollen feet and an injured eye

I have walked until my feet developed blisters on both my heels, which then burst and began to bleed as I continued to walk and hike and climb. Because there was no first aid available, the blisters developed into open sores that took more than three months to heal. The wounds would keep getting re-infected because we had to keep traveling from one church location to the next in order to stay on schedule. What can you do except believe God? You can't quit and go home, because these people are precious to God and they're depending on you for the Word. Sometimes while hiking, the pain in my feet would become almost unbearable. My traveling companions would many times look for a horse or carabao (the Filipino's beast of burden, used primarily to pull plows through the rice fields), so I could at least ride part of the way if the paths weren't too steep or dangerous. I'd get on the animal and hang on until it was time to dismount, because there were no saddles to sit in while riding. I was riding these animals bareback, and if you've ever seen pictures of a Philippine carabao, you can see how *wide* their back is. Riding on that beast of burden could be compared to doing cheerleading splits—for hours at a time! When I finally got off, I couldn't even straighten my legs for almost an hour. Not only were my feet swollen and bloody, but now I was bowlegged and without feeling below my hips!

I had to minister on these beat up feet. More than once, the sores would be so painful that I would have to sit while preaching and praying for the sick. They'd put a small wooden table up on the stage where the pulpit would normally go, and I'd sit on it and deliver my messages. We would have healing lines, where the sick would form a line and move along in front of me as I sat on the table laying hands on them as they passed. People would be saved and healed, but after the service my interpreter would have to help me off the table, out of the church, and into a chair, bench, or "bed" somewhere close. Then, he would sterilize a needle and proceed to puncture the infected blister wounds, draining the puss out each night before I went to bed. I was weak and dizzy for weeks, but whenever I would start to preach, the anointing would come and I would have God's strength to minister. Remember—no excuses for failure. Be strong, and do it!

During another one of my ten-week trips into the mountains and jungles, I scratched my eye while pushing through a heavy patch of thorn bushes. We were a party of about eight people, all walking through the thicket in a single file line. The guy in front of me pushed back the thorn bushes to walk through. Once he got clear he let the branch go, and it snapped back and raked me right across the right eye. Oh my God, did that hurt! It was pain like I had never experienced before in my life, and what's worse, I didn't know exactly how badly my eye had been injured. What are you going to do? Call the doctor? There are no phones, and there is no doctor anyway. There are no bandages, no medicine, no first aid kit to utilize—nothing. It's just you and seven or eight Filipinos who have left all to follow you.

Are you going to cry? Feel sorry for yourself? No, you can't do that. The strength of God constrained me, and even though my eye was obviously damaged and the pain was intense, I kept going. I put my hand over my eye because that gave me some relief from the pain. I started confessing the Word, praising God for my healing—while I kept walking, hiking, and climbing. Of course, all along the way, the devil sits on your shoulder, whispering lies in your ear, telling you you're going to lose the eye, you'll be blind forever, and things like that. Those lies keep coming, 24/7, like the fiery darts described in Ephesians 6. Since you don't even have a mirror to examine the injury, all you've got is your raw determination to trust God and God alone. He's telling you the injury isn't severe, but you've got no medical confirmation for that and the pain is just excruciating. Consistency of action is what produces the strength you need in times like these. Even if you have two swollen feet or one wounded eye (like me), you keep going because there are people up ahead who desperately need to hear from God, and He's depending upon you. I found that when you're strong, you will always consider the needs of others before you consider what is best for you.

I had to tough it out until the travel schedule was completed, and we came down out of the mountains to rest, regroup, and re-supply for the next adventure. In the case of my injured eye, when we finally got down to a coastal town where there was a doctor, he examined my eye and told me that I suffered a deep scratch across the surface of my eye. He then bandaged both my eyes and told me to go lie down at my interpreter's house for three days to rest. So off to "bed" I went to rest and recuperate, if you could call it that. My recuperation consisted of laying on an old wooden bed under a mosquito net for three days. I only got up to have someone help me to the bathroom when needed, and that was it. I'd come back to the bed, get under the net, and try to rest. The temperature was near 100 degrees F, there was no fan or air conditioner, and we were in a house that had a tin roof that got hot like a griddle when the sun came up. It was like laying in an oven during the day. Even though I was under a mosquito net, there were plenty of mosquitoes who got in and did their best to torment me.

So there I was, unable to see and unable to move about. Those three days without sight helped me to understand what it's like to be blind. Because of the heat, you're wearing clothing soaked in your own sweat and laying on a bed that's become wet with your sweat as well. During the day, it's the heat I had to deal with, but during the night, it's the mosquitoes, flies, and cockroaches. The mosquitoes would buzz around my ears all night, biting wherever they could, the flies would land at will, and I could feel the cockroaches crawling all over my body in the dark. Do you cry? Have a pity party? Do you feel sorry for yourself, or question God about why all of this is happening? If you're spiritually strong, you will do what Paul and Silas did in the jail at midnight. You'll lift your hands and begin praising God, like they did.

Acts 16:22–25

22 Then the multitude rose up together against them; and the magistrates tore off their clothes and commanded them to be beaten with rods.

23 And when they had laid many stripes on them, they threw them into prison, commanding the jailer to keep them securely.

24 Having received such a charge, he put them into the inner prison and fastened their feet in the stocks.

25 But at midnight Paul and Silas were praying and singing hymns to God, and the prisoners were listening to them.

They were beaten with rods, their backs had been whipped wide open, and they had been thrown into the deepest, darkest, and lowest pit in the jail. Their feet and hands are fast in the stocks, so they can't even move to find some relief from the pain caused by the injuries to their backs and bodies. And what are they doing at midnight? *Singing praises to God!* Is that a message, or what? Well, if they can do it, so can we. By experience, I know how hard it is on the flesh to praise God when your body is in great pain, but it's the strong thing to do. The strong Christian will praise God no matter what.

There are many powerful forces to deal with in places like the Philippines. There are witch doctors. There are voodoo and black magic worshippers. There are communist rebels and Muslim rebels with whom to contend. There are demon-possessed people walking the streets in every city, and even out in the countryside. When God sends you out to minister in places like this, you're going to need to be strong to do the work. If you aren't, the devil will eat you up and spit you out in a hurry. When God sends you up the mountain or into the jungle, you can't get by with playing church. If the devil doesn't get you, the water will!

On another occasion, while preaching up in the mountainous interior on the island of Cebu, I unexpectedly was confronted with a sorcerer and his demonic power. I had preached the salvation message with my interpreter and was laying hands on the people who had come forward for healing. Among those who came forward was a local witch doctor, but at the time, I didn't know he was a witch doctor who intended to do me harm. I thought he was a sick person like all the others, in need of healing. So when I came to him and asked what he wanted prayer for, he gave me some fictitious story about a condition he didn't have at all. I laid hands on him and prayed for his healing in Jesus' Name, and then went on to the next person in the line. When I laid hands on him, I felt nothing unusual at all, and had no idea who this man was or what he was intending to do. I had no vision, no inward witness, no word from the Lord—nothing.

Well, the meeting closed up and we left the market area. Later on, while we rested at the pastor's house, we found out who this man was and what he had tried to do. We discovered that the witch doctor's intention wasn't to receive healing, but to put a curse on me to kill me. He had pretended to be sick in order to get me to lay hands on him, because his plan was to transfer his evil power into my body when I laid my hands on him for prayer. This may sound strange to Western world ears, but this sort of thing is quite real—and can be quite deadly. God's power is transmitted through the laying on of hands, and the devil's power can be transmitted the same way—and this man knew it.

So, when I laid hands on this witch doctor, his intent was to curse me with his demonic power and kill me. How did we find all of this out? Because after I finished praying for him and moved on to the next person in line, this guy went throughout the whole marketplace, telling people that I was a powerful man of God. He told them to listen to what I had to say and to do what I told them to do because the power of God in me was greater than the demonic power in him. He told our crusade workers that when I laid hands on him, his power "went dead," as he put it—completely neutralized by the power of God in me. I never felt a thing, and had no idea any of this had taken place. I didn't even know what had happened until some of our crusade workers came to me at the pastor's parsonage after the service and told me this strange story.

That kind of divine protection doesn't come to us just because we're children of God. It comes because we take the time to make ourselves strong in the Lord. I know the importance of spiritual strength because I've been tested on the battlefield of world missions and have learned these things by experience. Anyone else who has stepped onto that kind of battlefield will attest to the truth of what I say. Even when we're not aware of some kind of spiritual attack against us, God is. If we've taken the time to prepare and be as strong as we can be in Christ, our level of strength will always be there to keep us safe and moving forward in the name of Jesus.

God calls Christians to a place of strength

As I have traveled extensively throughout the islands of the Philippines and all across the United States, I come into contact with many Christians from many different churches and groups. I find that no matter where I am, in Asia or North America or anywhere in between, the majority of these Christians are weak in spirit. That's why they whine and complain about how hard things are, or about how impossible things are, or about how they can't do this, or can't do that. Saints like that are easy prey for the devil, and that's a great tragedy because it shouldn't be that way, and doesn't have to be that way at all.

In fact, it should be the Christian tormenting the devil, rather than the devil tormenting the Christian. These spiritual principles will work for anyone anywhere. God is no respecter of persons. The Spirit of God is calling Christians worldwide into their rightful place of strength for these last days fights of faith. We must be strong and stay strong, not just for our benefit, but also for the benefit of those who don't know Jesus as Lord and Savior. Reaching many of these lost souls around the world will require a great deal of spiritual strength, which is exactly why this is such an important subject to understand and implement consistently. That's why several years ago God instructed me to use this catch phrase as often as we can wherever we go: *Be Strong! Stay Strong!* If we're to make any significant impact for Jesus in these end-times, we must get strong, and stay strong. We must do whatever is necessary to acquire the kind of strength needed to move mountains and subdue demons, but in addition, we must protect that level of strength once we get it.

As our Lord's return draws closer and closer, I believe Christians will have to decide to get strong and stay strong—or be left behind as we march forward in battle formation for the fights of faith ahead of us all. As the world continues to spiral out of control and fear usurps authority in the lives of untold millions on this planet, we Christians are going to have to "get strong for God or get out of the way." From what I have observed, lukewarm Christians will find no place in the end-time move of God's Spirit because their spiritual weakness will leave them too vulnerable to attacks from the devil. It's challenging enough to go on the offensive for God with all hands on deck, so to speak. But if we're spending all of our time tending to the weak and wounded because they weren't strong enough to carry their own weight on the battlefield, we won't be nearly as effective in winning the lost, making disciples of believers, and fulfilling the Great Commission. This is what has hindered the body of Christ all across the world from the time of Jesus until now, but praise God, I believe things are changing.

It's time to build up your level of spiritual strength. If you will take this message to heart and become a doer of what you learn (see James 1:22–25), consistently performing the seven priorities of life before the Lord, you'll be blessed in everything you say and do. You'll be strong, and you'll stay strong. If you will become consistent with doing and performing the seven priorities of life daily, you will become all you need to be, not just to survive, but thrive in Jesus. If you will take this message to heart, and become a doer of what you learn, you will be the kind of strong Christian God can use on the battlefields of life on earth. You will be truly "meet for the Master's use" (see 2 Timothy 2:21 KJV).

Consistently doing the seven priorities of life will earn you a place in God's elite army, and at that point, you'll look at yourself in the spiritual mirror, and wonder if the person you're looking at is really you. Consistency has that kind of transforming power, so make the decision today to access that power with a firm decision and daily commitment to performing the seven priorities of life.

CHAPTER FOUR

We are at war

2 Timothy 2:1–7

1 You therefore, my son, be strong in the grace that is in Christ Jesus.

2 And the things that you have heard from me among many witnesses, commit these to faithful men who will be able to teach others also.

3 You therefore must endure hardship as a good soldier of Jesus Christ.

4 No one engaged in warfare entangles himself with the affairs of this life, that he may please him who enlisted him as a soldier.

5 And also if anyone competes in athletics, he is not crowned unless he competes according to the rules.

6 The hardworking farmer must be first to partake of the crops.

7 Consider what I say, and may the Lord give you understanding in all things.

This passage of Scripture gives us a complete thought about spiritual strength in relation to spiritual warfare. By the Holy Spirit, Paul encourages us to consider his message and allow the Lord to give us spiritual understanding. In spite of God's specific instructions to consider what's being said here, I'm sorry to say that many Christians have never taken time to carefully consider the contents of these seven verses from 2 Timothy. That's a tragedy, because these verses contain some of the richest revelation on the subject of spiritual warfare that Christians desperately need to know about.

Verse 1 tells us to be strong in the grace that is in Christ Jesus. We are saved by grace and kept by grace, but here Paul is telling us we must be *strong in grace* also. Why? Because verses 3 and 4 tell us we're *soldiers at war*. A soldier cannot prevail in war unless he or she is very strong—period.

In verse 5, the NKJV version says that we're to *compete in athletics*, and when we do, we're to compete *according to the rules*. The KJV translation says it this way: *If a man also strive for masteries, yet is he not crowned, except he strive lawfully*. What does all of this mean? What does it mean to compete in athletics by competing according to the rules? What does it mean to strive for masteries lawfully so that we'll be crowned?

From the Greek, the word translated as "strive" in the KJV, or as "compete" in the NKJV, simply means to "work for, or to labor to attain something." What are we trying to obtain or to work for? The prize, or the reward, or the trophy—however you want to think of it. The Holy Spirit is telling us that this warfare is waged to obtain the prize, to win the fight, to earn our reward. That's what the athlete competes for, isn't it? The first place prize is what every athlete trains for and dreams about. That would be likened to the word "masteries" used in the original KJV translation.

You see, the one who is striving is the Christian. He or she is like the athlete competing for first place in whatever sport they participate. The word "masteries" represents the blessings of God promised to those who are in Christ, waging war on earth in the name of Jesus. The "crowning" takes place when we prevail in our fights of faith throughout life; being declared the "first place winner" by God against the attacks of the enemy.

This does not just pertain to the finish line either, as some might suggest. If you listen to some Bible teachers, you'll be left with the impression that the "masteries" or the "rewards" are only to be obtained at the end of this life, when we leave and go to heaven. We're told to expect nothing in this life but misery, heartache, struggle, frustration, and in general, spiritual defeat. But thank God, my Bible says something entirely different than that, and so does yours.

For the Christian, the "prize," the "reward," or the "masteries" represent all those wonderful things Jesus died and rose from the dead to provide for us all. Things like salvation, the baptism of the Holy Spirit with the evidence of speaking in tongues, healing and divine health, financial prosperity, deliverance, mental peace of mind, and so on. In fact, the prizes, rewards, medals or "masteries" we're to strive or compete to obtain are all the blessings already declared to be ours in Christ Jesus.

Ephesians 1:3

3 Blessed be the God and Father of our Lord Jesus Christ, who has blessed us with every spiritual blessing in the heavenly places in Christ.

Notice carefully the tense of this verse. It says God *has blessed us* with every spiritual blessing in the heavenlies in Christ Jesus. That's past tense, not future, and not even present. Past tense. That means it's already a done deal, as we say. When we're striving for the "masteries" or competing as an athlete for the first place prize, we're going for all the blessings God has already said are ours, but which the enemy is constantly trying to keep from us. In spiritual warfare therefore, obtaining the "masteries" and winning the prize is obtained when we release our faith, stand our ground, resist the devil, and appropriate every single blessing Jesus bled and died to provide.

So as we compare the KJV with the NKJV, we see that striving for masteries and competing in athletics are both the same thing, which is why newer translations render this passage that way. So we see that the Holy Spirit is using the field of athletics to illustrate principles that need to be applied in true spiritual warfare.

As an example, if a tennis player wants to win the tournament and be crowned champion, he must learn the rules of the game so he can master those rules and therefore "strive lawfully." He won't be able to win the match and be crowned champion unless he plays according to the rules of tennis. When he wins the tournament and has been crowned champion, he has obtained the "mastery," or the masteries, of that sport. But each sport has different sets of rules, so you have to know what rules apply to which sport. Otherwise you'll never be crowned champion, because you'll be forever confusing the rules of one sport with the rules of another, and that will never work. You can't play tennis by basketball rules any more than you can play soccer by rugby rules. Baseball and football are both popular American sports, but they play by completely different sets of rules. You must play by the rules of the sport you play if you expect to win.

The sport we Christians "play" is called the Great Commission. It's called winning souls. It's a "sport" that has definite rules—which must be understood and applied in order to prevail and be crowned the winner, or champion. If we expect to enjoy spiritual masteries to the fullest in this life, winning souls and enforcing the victory Jesus provided us, we must learn how to fight according to the rules established and revealed by God in His Word. You need to see the Bible for what it is, my friend—a legal law book and a military manual. It's other things of course, but first and foremost, it's our guide to practicing law before God and winning the fights of faith in which we engage the enemy on earth. We need to know these things because we're dealing with an enemy who is determined to keep us from winning our "match." That means he successfully neutralizes us and makes our lives of no importance or impact concerning the business of winning souls and changing lives on earth for God.

Salvation is a wonderful thing, but it's also a legal thing—instituted by a God who has rules of conduct firmly established because of His holiness, purity, righteousness, and so forth. Salvation didn't just happen in a haphazard way; the Old Testament law had to be established and then fulfilled, so that a New Testament law could be ratified before the Supreme court in heaven to take its place. Salvation wasn't purchased any old way; it was purchased because Jesus followed a very strict code of conduct and behavior, which earned Him the right to cancel our debt and pay the price for our sins.

Salvation is also a military handbook or manual. It shows us who our enemies are, what their tactics are, and how we engage them and prevail against them. God's command to fulfill the Great Commission doesn't happen without encountering intense resistance. Our enemies don't just step out of the way because we want them to. They move when we forcibly throw them out of the way. That's why you need to know how to "play by the rules."

We are at war

Whether you like it or not, you're on a planet that is embroiled in war. You've no doubt read the history books, where they talk about "World War I," and "World War II," but this war is far beyond the scope of those two world wars put together. The world war we fight is indeed global, affecting every human being on earth. There are no "neutral" countries in this conflict. There are no "conscientious objectors" in this fight. There are no places to hide and nowhere to go to avoid the conflict. There is nowhere you can go where the enemy won't find you. He's dedicated to killing and damning every single soul that has ever lived or is living now, and you better wake up to the reality of that.

Because of that, you're in this war whether you like it or not, by virtue of the fact you've been born. Believe it or not, some Christians think talk like this is foolishness, but I know from experience that it is not. This spiritual warfare is real and deadly. Losers in this war don't just get killed physically, or have their properties taken or destroyed, or suffer intense psychological trauma and emotional upheaval. We're not fighting for land, nations, continents, or to subject and conquer other people. We're fighting for the eternal souls of men, and losers in this conflict spend eternity in torment and indescribable suffering, with no hope of ever being rescued or redeemed.

Sobering, isn't it?

Satan is playing for keeps, and your soul is his target. Rules govern spiritual warfare the same way rules govern sports. In the arena of sports, victory doesn't come by luck, but by hard work, natural talent, knowing the rules of the game, and playing by them. We are dealing with enemies who are determined to keep the blessings of God away from us, and we can't defeat them in this life without engaging them in battle lawfully. You can't enjoy God's best unless you play by the rules that govern spiritual warfare. That is why it is so important to learn the rules that govern spiritual warfare. This is one war you can't win unless you play by the rules.

Do you know the rules?

God knows the rules, the devil and his demons know the rules, and we must know the rules, too. Our enemies, of which there are three, are very strong, and the only way we can out-muscle them is to have a working knowledge of the rules so we can be stronger ourselves. James 4:1–7 lists our three enemies in this life. They are 1) the devil, and the demons that work for him, 2) the world system that Satan is the god of and the controller of, and 3) our own bodies. Our ignorance of all of this is always our greatest handicap. Jesus has already defeated our enemies and given authority to us to not only live in victory over them, but to go into all the world and bring this saving knowledge to others. However, we will be contested all the time in many ways, so a failure to know and apply the spiritual rules that govern the conflict will hand the devil a huge advantage over us.

Victory in spiritual warfare does not come by luck any more than victory comes by luck to true champions in the arena of sports. Victory comes by hard work, and much of that hard work has to do with this business of being consistent with those seven priorities of life. This is one of the ways we apply the rules of warfare in combat. 2 Corinthians 2:11 says, "*Lest Satan should take advantage of us; for we are not ignorant of his devices.*" One of the first rules of spiritual warfare is to know the devil's tactics, tools, and devices. The devil's main weapon is deceit and deception. The truth is this: half the world doesn't believe the devil exists, and the other half lives under his bondage and oppression daily. That's how good he is at what he does. He convinces people first of all that he's not even real, and then if that doesn't work, he convinces them that he's not the cause or source of their problems. This is how he builds a very intricate but effective web of deceit in the lives of untold millions.

Not only is it how he is able to deceive multitudes worldwide, but how he deceives the believers as well. This is his number one way to offset the superior strength which we have as Christians. 1 John 4:4 tells us plainly that the Holy Spirit in us is greater than the devil who is in this world. We instantly have the advantage in spiritual warfare by virtue of the new birth, but have in a large measure given that advantage away through ignorance of what we're talking about here.

For example, if our missionary ministry needs more money, the first thing we should do is increase our giving. That's right—increase our giving. This is done for two reasons. First, because we're at war with evil forces that try to keep the flow of money away from our ministry, we increase our giving. Second, because the spiritual laws of prosperity dictate that we must first give abundantly before we can receive abundantly, we increase our giving. When we work the laws correctly, we get the money we need and win the battle at the same time.

Learn the laws and work the laws to beat the devil, his world system, and our dead-to-sin flesh. We Christians can't do it any old way and expect to win against an enemy that's been at this for a long, long time. Honestly, apart from God and a working knowledge of His rules and laws, we've got no chance against our enemies. I believe it's time to wake up to that fact. After more than two thousand years of having our teeth kicked in by the devil, you would think we'd begin to realize that doing things our way doesn't work. Trying to fight the devil in the arm of our own good intentions and sincere motives is like trying to fight against an army tank with a paintball gun.

We must learn to do things God's way, not our way. We will never beat the devil until we learn to apply God's laws to the conflict. The devil is strong, but we're stronger, so we can defeat him anytime we need to. Think about that for a moment. The devil, if he could, would kill every one of us in the next ten minutes, because he hates us as much as he hates God and wants every one of us to burn in hell forever and ever. But he cannot do it just because he wants to. He has to deceive us into giving him permission to destroy our lives, and sad to say, most men do this on a daily basis. How do they give him permission? Through ignorance of the conflict at hand and the rules that govern the conflict.

On the other hand, the moment a person decides to live free from the devil, the influence of the world system, or the flesh, what can the devil do to stop that from happening? Nothing! Of course he'll try, but in the end, if you're serious about victory, victory is yours. Why is that? Because in Christ, you're stronger than he is, so you can impose your will on him anytime you want.

Believers who know they're stronger than their enemies are halfway home to victory. At that point, all it takes to apply the second half of the "victory formula" is a working knowledge of the rules and spiritual laws that govern the warfare. Simply put—we cannot enjoy the advantages of having superior spiritual strength in Christ until we become consistent with our actions toward God. This is, as they say, where the "rubber meets the road." This is how we win the war and obtain the "masteries" which Jesus died to provide for us.

The law of replenishment

2 Timothy 2:6 says, "*The hardworking farmer must be first to partake of the crops.*" It doesn't say he should be a partaker, and it doesn't say he is entitled to be a partaker. The Word of God says "*the hardworking farmer must be a partaker.*" Must be! That's a command, not a request.

Why is it so important for the farmer to partake of his own fruits? Because one of the most important laws that govern spiritual warfare is the *law of replenishment*. This is a law that states that to get strong and maintain that strength, one must replenish spent spiritual energy with an equal amount of freshly imparted energy to maintain your current level of strength.

This law can be seen in operation in our natural world in many ways. For example, if you go out and work to dig a ditch in your front yard, you are expending physical energy. As long as you continue to feed your body the right amounts of food and water, you'll be able to keep digging. But what happens if you go on a prolonged fast, but still keep digging? What happens if you stop eating food and drinking fluids, but still keep digging? Sooner or later, depending upon how much strength with which you started, you'll collapse from exhaustion. Why? Because you stopped replenishing your spent energy with fresh energy.

This principle and spiritual law works exactly the same way in the spirit realm. Once again, understand that in context, the "farmer" of 2 Timothy chapter 2:1–7 is the Christian. In those seven verses, we find the believer described three ways. He's called a soldier, an athlete, and a farmer. So in context, the farmer planting his crops is also the athlete on the field playing his game, and the soldier on the battlefield engaging his enemies. As such then, the Christian must know and apply the law of replenishment if he is to overcome the enemies arrayed against him.

Spiritual energy is expended the same way physical energy is expended—through effort. We release spiritual force and energy when we use our faith to obtain the promises of God, standing our ground against the devil who seeks to keep those promises away from us. The more active you are for God, the more necessary it becomes to maintain a high level of strength against the devil. Active, aggressive, and passionate Christians become a bigger target for the enemy simply because they represent a bigger threat and can do more damage to the devil's kingdom on earth. So, in order to obtain and maintain a superior level of strength against the enemy, you must replenish spent spiritual force and energy with an equal or greater amount of fresh force and energy. You do that by feeding your spirit with the Word of God and being a doer of those seven spiritual priorities daily. That is spiritual law. It's not theory, it's law. It works the way it does and is beyond debate or question.

You know, someone can say that they don't believe they will fall if they jump off the roof, but they'll fall even if they don't believe they will. Why? Because it's a physical law—the law of gravity. A person's refusal to honor and respect that law doesn't change the fact the law works—every time. That's why its defined as a law; laws are applications that never change. We have the laws of mathematics, the laws of physics, the laws of chemistry, the laws of gravity, the laws of lift, the laws of thrust, and many others. We've defined these as laws because they operate by rules that never change. 2 + 2 is always 4. An airplane will always fly if you build it to a certain configuration, move it forward at a certain speed, and do certain things with rudders, pedals, and the like. How safe would you feel the next time you got on an airplane if the captain gets on the intercom before take-off to let you know that everyone on the flight deck hopes you get off the ground when you try to take off? No, the pilot gets on that intercom and with confidence talks about how you're going to take off, climb to a certain altitude, go in a certain direction, and land exactly where you paid to go. There's no fear about that because aviation is based upon laws that always work when you work them right.

Can you now see why the Holy Spirit defined strength as consistency of action? The consistent Christian is always replenishing himself, therefore he's always stronger than the enemy and can't be overwhelmed in some kind of surprise attack. He can never be overpowered because he never allows himself to run low on spiritual strength. He consistently keeps his spiritual "batteries" charged, maintaining a higher level of strength than that of the devil. Satan can never defeat a believer who does this.

Don't be caught off guard

In the Philippines, I once had a pastor friend whom I called and invited to my house for some lunch, prayer, and fellowship. I had obtained some good faith-building books from the States and wanted to give some of them to him to help him in his ministry. When he did not show up at the appointed time as scheduled, I wondered what had detained him. Normally, he was always such a punctual person, so not showing up was out of character for him. Even though I thought his no-show was odd, it didn't really worry me because I knew him and his wife to be dedicated, God-fearing people doing their best to pastor their church. I had conducted several extended meetings in his church, had spoken for him on Sunday many times, and they both had been my guests for lunch on several previous occasions. We had developed a warm and cordial friendship.

Three days later, some of the church members came to my house with an urgent request for me to come to the church and pray for this man's deliverance. At first, I thought they were joking, but soon saw they were very serious about their request. Even so, I couldn't believe what they were asking me to do. As I went back with them, I was still trying to process in my mind what they could possibly mean when they asked me to pray for his "deliverance."

When I arrived at the church, I could hardly believe my eyes! This pastor, my friend, whom I had known for several years as one of our good friends in ministry, was acting like a crazy man. He appeared to have totally lost his mind. He was speaking incoherently, drooling from his mouth, and making obscene gestures with his hands and body. His wife told me that he had been beating her and had actually tried to lock her in their parsonage. He had to be forcibly held down because he had been trying to bite anyone who came near him.

When one of his own church members tried unsuccessfully to restrain him, he rose up and bit me right in the chest. I had to literally slap him in the face to get him to loosen his grip. When I commanded the devil to depart in Jesus' Name, he shook his head violently from side to side and opened his mouth as wide as he could for as long as he could. Just a few days before this, my pastor friend was in my house, talking with me about the things of God. He had even set up a time when we would work together to pass out tracts with members of his youth department at church. I knew him to be a Bible-believing, tongue talking, full-Gospel, Pentecostal preacher. He was pastoring for one of the largest full-Gospel denominations in the world.

Even so, when the devil's surprise attack came, he was not able to withstand the concentrated onslaught of the enemy. The devil caught him off guard and ill prepared, and this was the result. A Christian cannot become possessed by the devil in spirit, but his or her mind, body, or both can be so overwhelmed by the enemy that the born-again spirit (with the Holy Spirit residing inside) loses all avenue of expression. This is what obviously happened to my friend, even though I could hardly believe it as I stood face to face with him in this condition.

I and all those with me ministered to this man for the better part of two days, but because he continued to have violent tendencies toward his wife, we admitted him into the hospital. The doctors doped him up for few days and then let him go when he seemed like he was back to normal. But as soon as he got back to the church parsonage, he started his tirades once again. Because he had become a public spectacle in the neighborhood, we asked his father to come from Manila and take him to a mental asylum in the southern part of the island of Mindanao, where this was taking place.

After treatment at the asylum and more than one year of rest at home, this man gradually recovered to full health. I was able to talk with him after his recovery was complete, and told me that he had been assigned to an assistant pastor's position in one of his denomination's churches in Manila. When I met him that day, he was so happy to see me and tell me all about his complete recovery. He shook my hand with joy and talked about the things of God with the same enthusiasm I had seen in him before this attack. He looked and sounded like the good friend I used to know. If you didn't know what had happened to him, you'd never think such a thing could've taken place, but it certainly did.

Well, all I can say is praise God for his victory. Deliverance doesn't always come instantly, but thank God when it does come. God's best is that we use our faith and gain the victory from the spiritual perspective, but if people need medicine, doctors, and physical therapy, then go for it. Whatever it takes is worth the effort if one seeks victory from enemy attack. But this experience for me underscores the truths I'm sharing with you. We don't know when the devil's next attack will be or how severe it will be when launched against us. Therefore, we must be consistent with the things of God so that we can maintain our edge and allow God the joy and privilege of tipping us off to what the devil may be planning. We may not know what the devil is up to, but God certainly knows. Through consistency of action, we can position ourselves with enough strength to not only resist the attacks when they come, but have the spiritual sensitivity to sense when something is about to be brought to bear against us. Then, when the next attack does come, we'll be ready and waiting.

The stakes in this spiritual warfare are the highest there can be. A man is an eternal spirit, and will spend eternity either with God in heaven or in hell with the devil. Hebrews 9:27 says, "It is appointed for men to die once, but after this the judgment." It doesn't say there are any "second chances" or "another life" to live to fix the mistakes made in this one. This life we live is literally a "once in a lifetime opportunity," so we must make the most of it and protect it with tenacity and passion. Once set, eternal judgment is forever. Not just for a few weeks or years, to teach the sinners a good lesson. That's not how God thinks or how God works, and you better realize that for your own soul's sake. He has very plainly laid out His plan for salvation and what it takes to enjoy the fruits of that plan. Heaven and hell are eternal places of abode, and it is our works and actions that determine which place we go to upon death, so this matter of spiritual warfare should never be taken lightly. Only a complete fool would take chances and play games with his own eternal soul.

I sometimes shake my head at those in the body of Christ who talk and act like this life is supposed to be one big Christian party. Spend time with many preachers and teachers, and they'll tell you that because Jesus died to give us abundant life (see John 10:10), we're supposed to buy up all we can, enjoy the world as best we can, and enjoy the "abundant life." Their definition of the "abundant life" is usually nothing more than greed and covetousness disguised as prosperity, and God hates it. Of course God promises prosperity, and I preach it, teach it, and believe in it without apology. But at the same time, these truths must be weighed and balanced with an understanding of what's actually going on down here on earth in the spirit realm.

We're at war, ladies and gentlemen! So if God is promising us the "abundant life," in the light of the reality of global spiritual warfare and the Great Commission given to us by Jesus Himself (see Mark 16:15–18), what would the prosperity be for and of what would the abundant life consist? Read your Bible, and you'll see clearly that in the context of global spiritual warfare, prosperity is promised for one reason—to win souls and finance the Great Commission. The abundant life isn't all about enjoying "things," but about being in position to change lives by the raw power of God. When we hold a crusade in the Philippines and some person who has never seen since birth has his eyes opened up by the power of God because we came with the saving message of the gospel—that's the true meaning of having an "abundant life."

The message that many preach about the abundant life is a very narrow-minded idea anyway, because it won't play well in many other parts of the world besides places like the United States. What do you think a Christian living in Communist China thinks about our supposed idea of the abundant life? What would the prosperity message mean to him? How about those in Muslim countries, where if caught, they have their heads cut off or their families ripped away from them, their houses burned down, and all property seized? I wonder what they would define as prosperity and the abundant life? Does that mean we should all trade in our cars, houses, and personal possessions, and live down at the YMCA? No, of course not. But it does mean you exercise faith for prosperity and the abundant life in light of the reality of war.

When you're engaged in war, you learn how to self-regulate if you're listening to the Spirit of God. If Christians would be more sober-minded about eternal matters, they wouldn't be wasting so much time, money, and energy enjoying their abundant life, whatever that means. They would easily recognize that the prime strategy of the devil and the world's system he operates and controls is to get us on the acquisition treadmill with everyone else, living out our lives in the vain pursuit of the newest gadget, thing, or toy. The Christian at war understands how meaningless the toys of the world are and knows they have no bearing upon what determines the eternal destinies of men.

Hell was created for the devil and his angels, not for men. But many humans will join the devil in hell because they took this war too lightly. As a soldier in the Army of the Lord, we should never be interested in anything this world has to offer. Remember those three enemies of James 4:1–7? The Bible tells us to learn to hate them with a *"perfect hatred,"* like David (see Psalms 139:21, 22). We all need to learn to hate the devil, hate his demons, hate sin, hate how sin destroys people's lives, hate the world system of greed and selfishness and spiritual deception and rebellion, and yes, hate the carnal nature of our flesh. Not just dislike them, or tolerate them—but hate them.

As an example, Paul talks about beating his own body black and blue in 1 Corinthians 9:27. He tells the Corinthians that he is "keeping his body under, in subjection to his spirit," lest that after he has preached to others, he himself would be cast off by God forever. Listen my friend, if the Apostle Paul feared being cast off by God forever, where does that leave you and me?

For the Christian soldier, fame, fortune and worldly acclaim should be an absolute joke. As soldiers of Christ, the only thing that should ever be of interest to us are the spiritual truths and laws that get us to a place of superior strength against our enemies and keep us there—for our own soul's sake and for the sake of those we're sent to minister to in Jesus' Name.

Be on the alert

Here is what Peter says about our enemy the devil.

1 Peter 5:8–9

8 Be sober, be vigilant; because your adversary the devil walks about like a roaring lion, seeking whom he may devour.

9 Resist him, steadfast in the faith, knowing that the same sufferings are experienced by your brotherhood in the world.

When armies go to battle, no soldier in his right mind takes the conflict lightly. He knows that taking his enemy lightly could cost him his life. Consequently, as he goes into battle, he's on the alert and ready at all times to defend himself and stay alive.

A smart soldier is constantly on guard against the enemy. Not only has he trained hard back in boot camp, but in addition he has studied his enemy's tactics and has learned how he thinks and acts. As a result, he's prepared for all contingencies. He knows what to do if his gun jams, even if it jams in the dark at night and there's no light to see. He knows how to defend himself in hand-to-hand combat. He knows what to do if trapped behind enemy lines. He knows all these things and more because he's spent the time to train hard and study his enemy thoroughly. Why all this effort? Because he's a soldier, and when it comes time for battle, his life is on the line. A smart soldier knows his life literally depends on living in a constant state of alertness when at war. If he didn't pay attention during the basic training or back at boot camp, chances are he won't last long against an experienced and battle-hardened enemy.

Ephesians 6:11–12

11 Put on the whole armor of God, that you may be able to stand against the wiles of the devil.

12 For we do not wrestle against flesh and blood, but against principalities, against powers, against the rulers of the darkness of this age, against spiritual hosts of wickedness in the heavenly places.

The word "wiles" in verse twelve means "strategies." The Bible says we must stand against the strategies of the devil. Satan is meticulous in his evil plans against us. His maneuvers are well thought out and no stone is left unturned in his attempts to damn your soul. This warfare is serious business to him, so it better be serious business to us as well.

Demon forces operate by rank

Demon forces operate by rank, just like soldiers in any army. There are *principalities*, then *powers*, then *rulers of the darkness of this age*, then *spiritual hosts of wickedness in the heavenly places*. Ultimately there is the devil himself as the commander-in-chief of this demonic army. Commands are given and orders are carried out. There are different levels of authority, but all the forces of evil are working with clockwork precision against you. Think of your life in terms of war, with a military mentality, and it will help you put these things in proper perspective. Never take Satan and his evil forces lightly. To do so is to invite spiritual disaster into your life.

Do you realize that while you sit reading this book, there are highly intelligent and organized forces at work to destroy your soul? Oh yes—absolutely! Espionage is a real part of warfare, and many times undercover intelligence makes the difference between victory and defeat. So—do you know the devil assigns his demons to follow you around gathering information he can use against you?

The devil is not all-knowing like God, so he assigns demons to gather information about you, just like any spy would do against his enemy in a time of war. These demon spies follow you around, listening to what you say and observing what you do. They want to know your likes and dislikes. They want to know how you get along with the rest of your family. They note who your friends are, what you read, what you watch, and how you entertain yourself. They observe you when you are with others and when you are by yourself in private. They stay with you because they're constantly probing and searching for your spiritual weak spots. They're looking for the holes in your armor, and they're patient while looking. Demons shadow people for weeks, months, or years, if necessary, patiently searching for anything that they could use against you to destroy your life and send you to hell.

Once these "spies" find something they think they can use against you, they go back to their superiors and report their findings. That's when they all sit down and draw up their plans against you, which when finalized, become the wiles of the devil—the demonic strategies launched against you. They discuss you at length, attempting to formulate the perfect attack—the one that will finally bring you down.

How can they best disguise their plan for as long as possible? When and where shall the attack be launched? Which demons are best qualified to carry out the attack? How quickly can they overwhelm you? How can as much damage as possible be inflicted in your life? Can the plan be executed quickly or will it take time to develop? How can the devil's forces overwhelm you before an effective defense is raised? How can the indwelling power of the Holy Spirit be neutralized when the attack is launched? How can they get you to make the wrong decisions that open the door and give them place in your life?

These are some of the many questions discussed by the devil's forces concerning you. These demons are not bumbling idiots. They're extremely intelligent beings with a great deal of patience and commitment to their cause. They'll patiently wait for years in some cases, waiting for the right time before launching their attack.

Never underestimate the enemy

Always remember this truth—Satan defeated Eve before she fell into sin. What does that mean? It means our enemy is extremely good at what he does. It means that he's a master of deception. It means you should never take him lightly, or underestimate his ability to do damage against you in your life. The Bible says that Adam and Eve were created with such brilliance that they were just "*a little bit lower*" than the Godhead (see Hebrews 2:7). Try to imagine how brilliant these two individuals were. Think of how great and glorious God is, and then try to understand that before sin came along, Adam and Eve were created with levels of intelligence and creative abilities that were just a bit below that of the Father, Son and Holy Spirit.

Yet, even with all that brilliance Adam and Eve had from God, Satan was still able to deceive Eve. Even with all the wisdom, knowledge, power and glory from God that Eve had upon creation, the devil was still able to trick her with deception. If the devil was able to come in and outsmart Eve in the Garden of Eden, how much easier is it for him to work his lies and deceptions against us? Adam and Eve were both far more intelligent than any of us are now in this fallen state of sin, and yet the devil was still able to come in and destroy everything. My friends, we need to wake up and become sober minded in this regard. We need to realize what kind of enemy we're facing. We need to understand how committed he is against us and what he is capable of doing to destroy our lives and damn our souls if we give him any place in our lives.

A smart military man will never take his enemy lightly, or underestimate his ability to wage war, do damage, or kill him. One of the first cardinal rules in military warfare is to never underestimate your enemy if you expect to enjoy victory. Even if their forces far outnumber those of the enemy, smart soldiers always plan the attack as if the enemy has equal or greater strength than their own. That is the wise way. It doesn't give place to the enemy unnecessarily. You'll never lose in battle by overestimating the enemy's capability against you, but you can certainly lose in battle by underestimating his capabilities.

The devil has a six-thousand-year head start on each of us in this generation, so let's not think for one minute that we've got the upper hand in this conflict apart from Jesus and consistency with the seven priorities of life. We're no match for the devil without God and obedience to His Word. Billions of souls are in hell forever today because they took their adversary too casually. Don't ever be guilty of making that same mistake!

CHAPTER FIVE

Don't entangle yourself

2 Timothy 2:4

4 No one engaged in warfare entangles himself with the affairs of this life, that he may please him who enlisted him as a soldier.

In this verse, the phrase "no one engaged in warfare" means you. In fact, it includes everybody, because no one is excluded from this spiritual warfare raging on earth today. It doesn't matter if you're saved or unsaved—you're in the war. It doesn't matter if you believe you're in the war or not—you're in the war. You're in the war whether you like it nor not, just by virtue of the fact you're here. Therefore, we all might as well deal with this fact.

Satan hates God but can't hurt God. He tried—and got kicked out of heaven so fast, Jesus compared it to a lightning strike on earth. (see Luke 10:18.) So because he can't hurt God, he goes after what God loves most—all of humankind. Man is God's crowning creation, which He loves more than anything else. Because of that, Satan is bound and determined to destroy and damn as many of us as he can. Because we're made in the image and likeness of God, Satan has made it his one and only goal to take as many of us to hell as possible.

That's why from the moment we take our first breath, the devil begins his plans and lays his strategies to deceive, destroy, and damn us to hell for all eternity. God has done all He can to make a way for us to accept Him and live with Him forever in heaven, and the devil continues to do all he can to prevent that. The good news is that as we accept the reality of all of this, we can go forth to battle knowing Jesus has already defeated the devil for us and stripped him of all his authority.

Matthew 28:18–20

18 And Jesus came and spoke to them, saying, "All authority has been given to Me in heaven and on earth.

19 Go therefore and make disciples of all the nations, baptizing them in the name of the Father and of the Son and of the Holy Spirit,

20 teaching them to observe all things that I have commanded you; and lo, I am with you always, even to the end of the age." Amen.

When Jesus died and rose from the dead, He took back all the authority from the devil that he originally took from Adam back in the garden of Eden. This passage emphasizes the fact that Satan no longer has any authority against you on earth. Jesus has it all. When Jesus said *all authority* has been given to Him in heaven and earth, it means exactly that! Praise God! Therefore, as you go forth to engage the enemy in spiritual conflict, remember that he has no authority to defeat you. Jesus took it all away from him when He rose from the dead (see Colossians 1:13 and Revelation 1:17,18). All the authority God gave Adam was surrendered to the devil when Adam and Eve sinned, but thank God Jesus got it back for all us. When He was about to leave to ascend back up into heaven, He plainly told us that this authority was being delegated to us on earth. When Jesus rose from the dead, He gave all His authority to the body of Christ on earth. Not part of it, but all of it. Ephesians 1:17–23 tells us that the spiritual body of Christ is comprised of Jesus as the Head, now seated in heaven at God's right hand, and us as the body, living our lives on earth in His Name, carrying out His commands to fulfill the Great Commission. As I said before, the body of Christ consists of believers who have died and gone to heaven, and the rest of us still living our lives down here on earth. Hebrews 12:1 describes the heavenly portion of the body of Christ as a *"great cloud of witnesses,"* who watch us and cheer us on from the grandstands of heaven.

This is why the devil's main tactic is to try to outsmart us and deceive us so that we won't use our God-given authority against him. Because he knows he can't out-muscle us anymore, he has to resort to deception and cunning craftiness. He tries to maneuver us into the position of using our own strength and authority to defeat ourselves.

Our free will is far more powerful than most of us have ever realized. In 2 Corinthians 4:4, Satan is called the god of this world system, but even sinners don't have to obey him if they don't want to. The devil hates all men, so it's never his will for even one of us to get saved. Yet when somebody decides to receive Jesus as Lord and personal Savior, what can the devil do to stop him? Nothing! Satan has to find a way around our free will in order to defeat us. The only way he can do this is to move us into a place where we allow him to defeat us without realizing what we're doing. In effect, we then are the ones defeating ourselves, because according to James 1:14, it's not the devil who forces us into sin. We do it to ourselves when we allow the devil, the world system, or the flesh to have place in our hearts, minds, and bodies.

So, how does the devil do what he does to steal, kill, and destroy? How does he get us to lay down our authority and accept defeat? One of the most effective ways is described in 2 Timothy 2:4—by becoming *"entangled in the affairs of this life."* The first thing, and the most important thing, to see in this verse is the fact that the devil isn't the one entangling us—we're doing it to ourselves. Yes, the devil can tempt us, and he does. Yes, the devil can try to influence us with the world's system, and he does. Yes, the flesh is constantly crying out for sinful expression, and it will continue to do so until its re-created by God's power (see 1 Corinthians 15:50–54). But even though all three of our enemies seek to gain entrance into our lives on a daily basis, they can't come in unless we let them! Therefore, if any man, woman, or child is spiritually defeated in this life, they have no one to blame for this but themselves. We can't blame the devil, although people love to do that because it absolves them of all responsibility. We can't blame God either, as much as people love to do that as well.

No, my friend, God won't force anyone to follow Him and live in victory over the devil while on earth, and the devil himself can't make anybody reject God and die lost against their free will. It just doesn't work that way. Man has a free will, and can make choices. Therefore, we must recognize all the tactics, plans, and strategies of the enemies of our soul, so that we constantly make the right choices, not the wrong ones. Believe me when I tell you, if you chose to give the devil, the world's system, or your flesh a place in your life, they'll jump at the opportunity to come in and destroy you.

What are "the affairs of this life"?_____

When the Bible tells us to avoid the "affairs of this life," what does that mean? It means anything and everything we have to do just because we're living on earth on a day-to-day basis. Notice it talks about the affairs of this life. That means the time we spend on earth in these earthly bodies. And the "affairs" of this life deal with the everyday routines of life: cooking, cleaning, shopping, washing clothes, ironing, cutting the grass, edging the lawn, weeding in the garden, washing the car, taking care of the house and fixing it up when necessary, going to work, going to school, raising a family, feeding the kids, spending quality time with your spouse, taking care of the baby, playing with the children, taking vacations, going to gym for workouts, watching TV, surfing the Internet, going to the ballpark, or playing a round of golf on the weekend. Everything from ministry to work to family to education to career to hobbies to whatever—these are all the things that comprise what the Bible calls the affairs of this life.

Since the Bible also says not to become entangled in the affairs of this life, we need to understand what an entanglement is. When I sought the Lord for a definition for the word "entanglement," this is how He defined it for me: *An entanglement is anything that prevents you from fulfilling your spiritual priorities every day.*

First of all, please notice the word "anything" and the term "every day." We all need to understand their importance if we're to successfully wage war in the Name of Jesus on earth in this life.

"Anything" refers to the affairs of this life—no matter what they may be. Any of the affairs of this life can become an entanglement to you. It doesn't have to be something bad or sinful. In fact, most of the affairs of this life aren't sinful at all. They are things we have to do, day in and day out—the routines of life. But if these routines or activities prevent you from fulfilling your seven priorities of life each day, those routines or activities become entanglements to you.

"Every day" has to do with the issue of consistency of action. Performing the seven priorities of life once in a while in not good enough. Performing them only on Sundays, or only when we feel spiritually inspired won't cut it. Whatever you do that prevents you from being consistent with these spiritual priorities becomes an entanglement to you.

God knows you have to take care of the affairs of this life. He's not expecting us to go live in a cave somewhere or join a cloistered religious order and live behind the wall in some monastery in Europe. He knows people have to eat, sleep, and earn a living. He understands these things better than anyone. He knows you must devote time to your marriage and family—in fact He's the one telling us we need to do those things. God knows there are thousands of things that need to be done every day, and He doesn't expect us to drop everything and stop living so we can become "spiritual." However, you need to know there is a vast difference between taking care of the affairs of life, and becoming entangled in them.

Two types of entanglements

In order to recognize and avoid the temptation to become entangled in the affairs of this life, we must understand that there are two basic types of entanglements. Here's what Hebrews says about this:

Hebrews 12:1–2

1 Therefore we also, since we are surrounded by so great a cloud of witnesses, let us lay aside every weight, and the sin which so easily ensnares us, and let us run with endurance the race that is set before us,

2 looking unto Jesus, the author and finisher of our faith, who for the joy that was set before Him endured the cross, despising the shame, and has sat down at the right hand of the throne of God.

In these two verses, we see the two kinds of entanglements. They are *weights* and *sins*, and they are not the same. If they were the same it would be worded this way: "Let us lay aside every weight, *which is* the sin that so easily besets us." But it doesn't read that way, does it? So, first of all, recognize the two different kinds of entanglements. They are weights first, and sins second. The Bible tells us to "*lay aside*" both of them if we're to run our race and reach the finish line for Jesus. Running the race deals with the effective day-to-day management of our time, wherein we make the right scriptural choices that consistently reject temptation and keep our eyes focused on Jesus, the author and finisher of our faith. Reaching the finish line deals with our triumphant exit from Planet Earth—either through death (on God's timetable—not the devil's) or via the Rapture, whichever event precedes the other.

Notice again that we do the laying aside—not God, not the angels, not our friends, our pastor, or some minister on TV. If we want to live victoriously and fight in this war successfully for God, we're going to have to discipline ourselves to lay aside both the weights and sins that so easily gain entrance into our lives. I can't do this for you, and you can't do this for me. We're each responsible for this in our own lives.

Your pastor can't do this for you. Some evangelist can't do this for you. Neither can Dr. Raymond T. Radio, Reverend Tommy Television or Bishop Best-seller. We lay aside the weights, and we lay aside the sins that come against us daily.

Weights and sins don't come along and jump on you against your will. Yes, temptations will surely come to try and get you to open the door and let them in, but in the end, you are the only one who can open that door. Listen to what God says about this:

Isaiah 54:14–17

14   In righteousness you shall be established;
     You shall be far from oppression, for you shall not fear;
     And from terror, for it shall not come near you.

15   Indeed they shall surely assemble, but not because of Me.
     Whoever assembles against you shall fall for your sake.

16   "Behold, I have created the blacksmith
     Who blows the coals in the fire,
     Who brings forth an instrument for his work;
     And I have created the spoiler to destroy.

17   No weapon formed against you shall prosper,
     And every tongue which rises against you in judgment
     You shall condemn.
     This is the heritage of the servants of the Lord,
     And their righteousness is from Me,"
     Says the Lord.

In this passage, God shows us how the whole thing works when it comes to temptations against us, where they come from and how to get rid of them. When we accept Jesus as Lord and personal Savior, we become the righteousness of God in Christ (see 2 Corinthians 5:21). We become, as verse 14 says, established in righteousness. As such, we are established in Christ at God's right hand, spiritually speaking, and are far from oppression, fear and terror.

But notice the oppression, fear, and terror will still try to come to the righteous children of God, but we don't have to accept their invitation. In verse 15, God says they will surely assemble against you, but they're not coming from Him. In other words, God is not the one bringing the oppression, fear and terror against you. Well, if they're not from God, they have to be from someone else, right? I'll give you three guesses who that mystery attacker might be. Verse 16 says they're all from the "spoiler" who wishes to destroy you. The spoiler is not God—it's the devil. God doesn't come along to spoil or destroy anybody—He so loved the world He sent Jesus to die for all of us. It's the devil who tries to destroy us, oppress us, terrorize us, and damn us. It's God who wants to save us and protect us all the days of our lives. This is a very simple truth, but many have allowed the devil to warp the scriptures in this passage, and in others too, convincing many that God is the source of their problems, when all along it's the devil who is their real problem.

In Acts 10:38, the Bible says that Jesus went around "*doing good, and healing all oppressed by the devil, for God was with Him.*" That one verse right there is as simple and as easy-to-understand as any could be.

Many people have misunderstood verse 16 above, thinking that God created the devil specifically to spoil and destroy men's lives, but nothing could be further from the truth. This verse must first of all be understood in light of all the other verses on this subject from Genesis to Revelation. When that is done, the obvious conclusion is that God never created the spoiler to destroy us, as this rendering might suggest.

In fact, many Hebrew scholars tell us that this verse, and others like it, especially in the Old Testament, should have been translated in the permissive sense, rather than in the causative sense. In other words, many things that people think God causes are actually only what God permits.

God didn't create Satan as he is today. He was originally created as Lucifer, who was so beautiful, the original King James translation says he "sealed up the sum," which means he was beautiful beyond words (see Isaiah 14:12–15 and Ezekiel 28:11–18 KJV). God didn't create Satan—Satan created Satan. He was created originally as Lucifer, but became the devil when he actually invented sin and iniquity within himself. When God talks about creating the "spoiler who destroys," in context, He's reminding us that even though He was Lucifer's creator, He allowed him to become warped and sinful in the same way He allows any of us to choose between right and wrong. Therefore, although He wasn't responsible for how Lucifer became Satan, God is reminding us that in Christ, all the authority needed to subdue our enemy is ours, and that no weapon formed against us can ever prosper if we don't allow it, as it states plainly in verse 17. Finally notice also that in verse 17, we're told that we're the ones who condemn and judge those who come against us—not God. That's authority. That's dominion. That's who we are now in Christ at God's right hand. No weapon formed against us can ever prosper or be successful, as long as we become strong and stay strong through consistency.

We have the God-given authority to change course in our lives anytime we get serious about it. We can put on the weights, and we can take them off. We can enter into sin, and we can repent and renounce sin. It's all up to us. In other words, whatever the mess is that we got ourselves into because of bad choices is the same mess we can leave behind if we choose to exercise our authority, perform our seven priorities of life daily, and kick the devil off our doorstep. Of course, God is there to help us because we'll need His guidance and direction in the midst of the battles. Remember our authority is only as good as the Power that backs that authority. Don't go off thinking you're so good you don't need God. He's forever the vine, and we're forever the branch. Don't forget that, because spiritual pride is the very sin that caused Lucifer to morph into Satan. At the end of the day, it's our responsibility to throw off the weights and get rid of the sin in our lives. It's not God's responsibility for you, it's yours and yours alone. If you do your part, God will do His part. If you do what you can do, God will do what you can't do. If you choose to exercise your authority, get and become strong in Christ, and no longer tolerate compromise with weights or sins, God will stand with you and behind you with the power to make good on your faith declarations.

We find a perfect example of this in the book of Deuteronomy, when the Jews were about to enter the Promised Land.

Deuteronomy 9:1–3

1 "Hear, O Israel: You are to cross over the Jordan today, and go in to dispossess nations greater and mightier than yourself, cities great and fortified up to heaven,

2 a people great and tall, the descendants of the Anakim, whom you know, and of whom you heard it said, 'Who can stand before the descendants of Anak?'

3 Therefore understand today that the Lord your God is He who goes over before you as a consuming fire. He will destroy them and bring them down before you; so you shall drive them out and destroy them quickly, as the Lord has said to you."

As we read this passage, understand that this is the second time the Jews stood on that spot to cross the river Jordan. They had stood there forty years earlier, but they blew it through unbelief, and as a result, wound up wandering in the wilderness for forty years. If you study chapters 13 and 14 of the Book of Numbers, you will see that the Israelites blew it because they were afraid of the giants they saw when they went over to spy out the land.

To be sure, those giants were huge, fierce, and intimidating from the natural standpoint. If you run cross references, you'll find that Goliath, the giant David killed later on after this, came from this tribe of people—a tribe called the Anakim. They were Goliath's ancestors. Now realize that Goliath was only one man, yet when the armies of King Saul saw him, they fled in stark terror. You can imagine how imposing he was. Saul and his men were all seasoned soldiers themselves, having fought numerous times on battle-fields, but they'd never seen a man that big. When Goliath challenged them to pick one man to come and fight with him to the death, they all ran and hid behind the rocks and trees. Nobody had the courage to face this man alone in mortal combat, because nobody thought they had a chance against a soldier so huge and intimidating.

In case you need to appreciate the size of this one man, let me help you. The Bible says Goliath measured somewhere between nine-and-a-half and eleven feet tall, depending on the cubit measurement used. Think about that for a moment. The tallest of all professional basketball players are never more than seven or seven-and-a-half feet tall, which tells us this man was at least two or even four feet taller. He wasn't some scrawny, skinny guy either. He was, as Saul said himself, a warrior from his youth. His upper-body armor alone weighed one hundred twenty-five pounds. He wore a bronze helmet and bronze leg guards, and his armor bearer stood in front of him, so it was actually two men and not just one. It was Goliath, and his armor bearer. Like I said, when Saul and his army took one look at this man, they ran for cover.

Now when the twelve spies went into the Promised Land, they didn't find just one man like Goliath over there—they found a whole tribe of them. The Israelite spies took one look at the children of Anak, and their faith in God's covenant with them went right out the window. When it did, so did their chance to ever cross over and take possession of God's Promised Land. The price for their unbelief was a forty-year stretch wandering around in the desert as every man above the age of twenty died off. Now, forty years later, here we see them standing on the same spot as before, and God has some very pointed things to say to them.

When the Jews stood at the Jordan River for the second time, God plainly told them that the giants were still over there on the other side. Furthermore, He told them that their cities were still great and walled up to heaven. He told them these were the fierce giants they had heard so much about all their lives—people so fierce and overwhelming that nobody could ever stand successfully against them. To put the icing on the cake, the Lord said the people living over there were still, to a man, mightier and stronger than the Israelites. Let it never be said that God pulls any punches, or holds back the truth. He told the Jews exactly what they were going to have to face, and that in the natural—there was no hope and no way.

But all of that was from the carnal standpoint, and God was quick to declare the "flip side" to this issue—the spiritual side of faith. Reminding the Jews to consider the spiritual side of things, God told His people that He would go over ahead of them as a consuming fire to destroy their enemies and bring them down to defeat. But there was only one small catch: the Jews had to cross the river, go over there and engage them in battle to drive them out. God would consume their enemies, destroy them and get rid of them, but only after the Israelites went over and faced them in battle to drive them out. It's not all about God, and it's not all about you—it's about us working with God in partnership. We do what we can, and then He does what we can't. Simple. We can kick the devil out, and He can enforce that decision.

Simple. What can the devil do about it? Nothing—except try to pick a soft spot to land on after you give him the boot.

It's the same for us today as it was for them, and it's been for anybody since the beginning when God gave Adam and Eve dominion on earth (see Genesis 1:26–28). So many Christians are on the outside looking in, wondering why their lives are in such a mess. They sit around at home, depressed, confused, disillusioned, and feeling sorry for themselves. Poor old me! They hold big pity parties for themselves and invite everyone to come to the party and feel sorry for their plight in life. They take their anti-depressant pills, their sleeping pills, and their migraine headache pills. They keep waiting for God to send someone along to deliver them. They keep waiting for God, hoping that one day He'll drive the devil out of their lives. But God isn't going to do one thing about the devil because He's already done everything that needs to be done. Jesus has already risen from the dead, stripped the devil of all authority, and given that authority to us on earth. So, as long as people sit there with all their feel-sorry-for-me moods and melancholic behavior, the devil will sit next to them and keep giving them Kleenex.

God isn't going to drive the devil out—He already told us to do it in His Name. So, if this depressed, defeated, and confused person sounds like you today, I've got a "word" for you from God. Go to your closet, put on your gospel boots, and kick the devil right out the back door. But if you have that kind of desire—to be the "kicker" instead of the "kickee," you'd better get rid of the weights and sins. If you expect to have the strength and courage to confront the devil and throw him out of your house and home, you cannot allow yourself to become entangled in the affairs of this life.

Deal with the sin

When the Lord was talking to me about the differences between weights and sins, He told me that in most cases, His children don't have as much of a problem with sin as they do with weights. So, for the purposes of this book, I'm not going to spend time talking about the issue of sin, other than to say that if you're in sin, get out of sin today. Get rid of that sinful baggage in your life, because as we've already seen, time is short. Sin is willful rebellion against God and His Word, and it can be expressed through actions, words or thoughts. So if you're words are wrong, if your actions and choices in life are wrong, and if your thoughts are wrong, repent before God, and receive forgiveness. Then, start doing what this book is telling you to do—get strong and stay strong through consistent performance of the seven priorities of life. Doing that will elevate your spirit man to a place where you're strong enough to both recognize and resist sin when it comes to tempt you.

The wages of sin is death (see Romans 6:23), and death is definitely an entanglement. Deal with sin now—today—and let the Lord wash it away by His shed blood on heaven's mercy seat.

Shed the weights

People who love the Lord want to please Him by staying free from sin. They have a genuine desire to live right and stay clean. However, so many of them still struggle with the weights, and this is what the Lord emphasized to me when we talked on these things. Weights can cause the most dedicated and hardworking of Christians to get tripped up. The man who seeks to please God is going to do his best to stay away from sin. If not, I would openly wonder if that person was ever truly saved in the first place. When one is truly born again, and has become a new creature in Christ (see 2 Corinthians 5:17), the "want-to" for sin disappears. If they do make a mistake and fall into sin, they're quick to go to God, repent, stand on God's Word, receive their forgiveness and move on.

1 John 1:9

9 If we confess our sins, He is faithful and just to forgive us our sins and to cleanse us from all unrighteousness.

If sin is the issue, a true believer who has been taught correctly will know to stand upon his righteousness in Christ to repent, receive forgiveness, and move on without any condemnation. So the sin problem can be solved with repentance and the forsaking thereof. But how about the weight problem? First of all, let's once again define the term. As I sought the Lord again in prayer, I asked for a definition for what a spiritual weight would be. Here's His definition:

A weight is anything that steals your time. In and of itself it is not a sin, but it becomes a weight because it steals the time you need to perform the seven priorities of life.

In other words, by stealing your time away from God, these weights slow you down and cause you to be less effective against your enemy in the spiritual warfare with which we're involved. This is exactly what he wants, and what he tirelessly works to achieve against us—all of us.

If you're not careful, the affairs of this life will weigh you down spiritually. Even if sin is not the issue, realize that weights alone can still do tremendous damage in your life. They can weigh you down so far and so fast, before you even realize what is happening. The more time you devote to the affairs of this life, the more those things will weigh you down and sap your spiritual strength. When you fail to consistently set time aside daily to perform those seven priorities, your level of spiritual strength goes down proportionate to the degree of your spiritual laziness and neglect. This is precisely what the devil wants to see happen. If he can't just get you to sin outright, he'll work on you from this other angle. If sin has no place in your life to any significant or habitual degree, Satan will go to work to try and get you weighed down with so many weights, you can no longer run your race effectively for God. At that point, you may be living a sin-free life before God, but in terms of battlefield presence, you've become nothing more than a casualty of war. How can God count on you under fire when you're so weighed down you can't even get off the bed back at the M*A*S*H tent?

Remember in context, Hebrews 12:1 talks about a runner running a race. When was the last time you saw a runner putting on as much weight as possible before he stepped out on the track to run the race? It's quite the opposite, isn't it? Runners don't put on as much weight as they can, they take off as much weight as they can to run the fastest race possible. How stupid would it look for a sprinter or hurdler to strap on as much weight as possible to make themselves as heavy as possible, and then wonder in amazement as to why he finished last? You'd think the guy had lost his mind, right? Well, in the spirit realm, that's exactly what happens when Christians try to run their race for God while continuing to put more and more weights on their back. If that has been you, get rid of those weights in Jesus' Name.

We are ambassadors for Christ in every area of life—physical as well as spiritual—so we must not neglect the affairs of this life. Yes, we must be spiritual for the Lord's work, but not at the expense of becoming a stumbling block in this world. We need to take care of the affairs of this life because we represent the King of Kings and Lord of Lords. It's our responsibility as children of God to always look our best, act our best, and keep our lives as organized and as efficient as possible. Even though we're spirits, we're living in physical bodies on earth in this life, so we must always keep proper perspective and balance our lives according to the guidelines found in God's Word.

Take care of the affairs of this life, but don't become entangled with them. Don't let sin have any place in your life, and don't get weighed down with the everyday things that rob you of the time needed to perform the seven priorities. The more sin or weight allowed in your life, the weaker you become spiritually. There is nothing wrong with the affairs of this life, but problems arise when we give them priority over the seven priorities: worship, praise, prayer, confession, meditation, study and reading, and sharing. Put these things first and foremost over everything else, and things will go well for you on a consistent basis.

Remember the Law of Replenishment, one of the most important of all the laws governing spiritual warfare. The hardworking farmer must be first to partake of the crops, as it tells us in 2 Timothy 2:6. The farmer must partake of his own harvest if he is to maintain the strength needed to keep on working. Satan knows this, and that's why he tries to keep you busy with the affairs of this life. If you have no time to devote to the seven priorities of life, the devil has successfully moved you into a position of entanglement. As long as you're in that situation, you will never have enough strength to beat the devil and walk triumphantly in this warfare. He'll be able to overpower you and have his way against you in this life, and that's never a good thing.

Stay away from entanglements

Entanglements keep you from being consistent with the seven priorities of life, and you need to be doing all seven of them daily to keep yourself built up and strong for the fights of faith today and the battles that await you in the future. There will never come a time in this life when the devil will leave you alone. Every day and every step of the way, we will be contested by the enemy. That's the way it is, so get a reality check today and make the necessary adjustments to bring yourself to that wonderful place of spiritual strength and superiority over the devil, his world system, and our dead-to-sin bodies.

Consistency is the key to making all of this work to your advantage. Every day, choose to put God first. Before your marriage, before your kids, before your job, your career, or your education. Spending time with God is more important than wasting time watching TV, chatting and texting with friends, or surfing the Internet. It's okay to buy tickets and go see your favorite team play down at the stadium or ballpark, but just be sure you've given God your best first, by performing those seven priorities faithfully each day. Then by all means, go enjoy the ball game—and have a hot dog for me.

Everything we do takes time because we live in a time-bound dimension. The seven priorities of life take time to perform, and so do the affairs of this life. It's all a matter of choice. Consistent Christians know how to use their time wisely because they know that wasted time equals lost spiritual strength. To win our fights of faith against our enemies, we must learn how to utilize our time to the utmost. Wasted time is a sin against God, and against those we're charged to go to in the Name of Jesus.

CHAPTER SIX

Victory demands time management

Ephesians 5:15–16

15 See then that you walk circumspectly, not as fools but as wise,

16 redeeming the time, because the days are evil.

Colossians 4:5–6

5 Walk in wisdom toward those who are outside, redeeming the time.

6 Let your speech always be with grace, seasoned with salt, that you may know how you ought to answer each one.

1 Peter 1:17

17 And if you call on the Father, who without partiality judges according to each one's work, conduct yourselves throughout the time of your stay here in fear;

Throughout the Bible, there are many scriptures like these regarding time. As an example, Psalms 90:12 tells us to number our days to gain a heart of wisdom. In the passages above, we again see the emphasis upon time management. To put it bluntly: time management is a necessity if you expect to live a consistently strong life here on earth, because this earthly life is governed by time. God has chosen to govern this world, or this dimension, using time blocks that are called seconds, minutes, hours, days, weeks, months and years. He has given us the responsibility to manage that time wisely, which is the heart of wisdom talked about in Isaiah 33:6.

When the Word of God tells us to "redeem" the time, it means we make the most of the time that is available to us each day. Wasted time is a sin. The consistent Christian has become strong because he or she has learned how to "pass the time" of sojourning on earth in fear of the Lord. Strong Christians don't waste their time because they know the enemy is not bound by time. Human beings live in this physical dimension and are bound by time, but those who live in the spiritual dimension are not. That's why we must learn to make time work for us instead of against us. We do that when we faithfully perform the seven priorities of life daily.

All of us must take care of the affairs of this life, but the consistent Christian will keep his time allotted properly and scripturally. The majority of his time will be spent performing the seven priorities of life, while the time spent taking care of the affairs of this life will be kept to a bare minimum. This is important because time is precious, valuable, and a gift from God. Each day is God's gift to you, and that day is governed by time.

Wise Christians understand the fact that the devil has a time advantage on us every day. Why? Because, as an example, he has no need to sleep as we do. He doesn't live in a body that requires it. In addition, Satan doesn't have to eat food as we do, or any of the other things that comprise the affairs of this life. The devil has no need to devote time and energy to a marriage and a family, but we who are married with kids certainly do. The point is this: while we are busy taking care of the affairs of this life, Satan is out there—with no time constraints—working on his plans against us. In fact, the devil has a six- to eight-hour time advantage on us each day just because our bodies require that kind of time for sleeping. And once we wake up and get up, there are all those many things that must be done—called the affairs of this life.

While we're so busy running around town taking care of the affairs of this life, Satan is out there forming his strategies against us. As an example, how much time do we spend going to school if we're still in school? Depending upon what level of schooling we're talking about, it could be as much as eight to ten hours a day, five days a week. Our two children would rise at 5:15 a.m. every school day, catch the bus at around 6:20 a.m., and we wouldn't see them again until around 4:30 p.m. later that afternoon. This was their schedule all through middle school and high school. Well, the devil doesn't need to educate himself, work for a diploma, or go out and earn a paycheck to pay for things.

With these several examples, can you see with me that our enemy enjoys a time advantage simply because he's a spirit operating in a timeless dimension, while we're spirits living in bodies governed and regulated by time? The devil has a full twenty-four hours each day to devote to finding ways to kill you, hurt you, or destroy you. He doesn't get tired, needs no lunch break, and doesn't want or need a vacation. He's not constrained by a physical body like we are, therefore he doesn't have to eat, sleep, rest, workout or any of the other things related to good health and physical fitness. We have to do all those things, but he does not. He's a spirit, operating out of the spirit world, but trying to dominate and control us in this physical world. Are you beginning to realize how precious time is, and how important it is to manage time each day?

Television is one of the biggest time stealers available to the devil against us. If we sit down to watch a TV program, how much time is being spent doing so? Thirty minutes, sixty minutes or longer? Rather than watching some movie, some sitcom, some police drama or news show, we could be using that time to perform some of the priorities of life. But in most cases we don't see things that way, do we? The "need" for entertainment outweighs the importance of keeping your spirit strong, so for most believers, the TV wins out night after night. Does watching news programs hour after hour edify our spirit man? Hardly! Do we need to see our favorite TV shows day after day, or week after week? Of course not. Does watching reruns of movies we've already seen a thousand times constitute a wise use of time? No. For so many Christians, from the time they wake up until the time they go to bed, the TV is on, and it is the center of their world. This only plays into the hands of the devil—it certainly doesn't do much to get us strong and keep us strong in the Lord.

Remember the definition for what a "weight" is. Watching TV is not a sin in and of itself, but if we haven't taken time that day to spend with God in the performance of our seven priorities of life, we've allowed our TV viewing to become an entanglement. If we haven't put God first, we've got no business in front of that television set. Also remember this one great truth about time management: *The top priority is to keep the top priority the top priority*. Watching TV all day long is not your priority as a Christian soldier in the army of the Lord. Being strong and staying strong is.

Television becomes a weight because it robs us of time that should have been spent building up our spirit man on the inside. Can you see that? Even in my own life as a traveling minister, I must constantly resist the temptation to sit in my hotel room in between services and watch TV. Ever since 1980, I've traveled almost every weekend in ministry, speaking and ministering in churches all over the U.S. and the Philippines. In most cases, I stay in hotels when on the road, and it's amazing how much of a temptation it can be to come into that room, and plop down on the chair or bed, and start channel surfing. You're doing it before you even realize you're doing it, and just like that, three or four hours have passed and you've done nothing that can help you keep your edge for the Lord. Do any of you know what I'm talking about?

Those three or four hours could've been used to pray, study my Bible, wait upon the Lord, or something else that would strengthen me and keep me as strong as I need to be as an apostle and front-line fighter in God's army. You can be sure the devil isn't taking a three- or four-hour coffee break, waiting for me to get my spiritual act together. While I'm wasting time in that hotel room watching some dumb show of some kind, the devil is always out there, planning his next attack against me. Therefore, I must live a better-managed day for my sake, the Lord's sake, my family's sake, and our ministry's sake. So do you, and so do all of us who call ourselves Christians. It's just that simple my friend.

Each and every day, put the seven priorities of life where they ought to be—first place. Learn to be a consistent Christian and use your time wisely. Put God first each day by faithfully performing each of those seven priorities—then comes your marriage and family affairs, followed by your job, school, career or ministry, with leisure pursuits bringing up the rear. Time-wise, this is how you should prioritize your day. Keep your priorities straight each day, and you'll soon find that time will be working for you instead of working against you.

In this spiritual warfare, our enemies are either going to grind us into the ground, or we're going to grind them into the ground. It's going to be one or the other—there is no middle ground. Satan is very dedicated and consistent in using time to war against us, so we must be as dedicated and consistent in using time to our advantage in our fights of faith against him. Instead of getting bogged down with all kinds of entanglements, the wise and strong Christian stays focused and on task for the Lord. Doing the seven priorities of life daily is one of the best ways to do that.

Colossians 3:1, 2

1 If then you were raised with Christ, seek those things which are above, where Christ is, sitting at the right hand of God.

2 Set your mind on things above, not on things on the earth.

When we're told to set our minds on things "above," we're being told to spend time pursuing or doing things that will build us up spiritually. We're being told not to waste our time, but to manage it wisely for the glory of God, and for the work of ministry. We're being told to get strong and stay strong through consistency. We're being prepared and trained for the next surprise attack against us. It doesn't matter what the devil may have up his sleeve against you. If you've set your mind on things above consistently, he'll never be able to catch you off guard or unprepared to resist him when he comes against you.

Dealing with demons

Once I was holding a four-day crusade in a small town called Jimalalud, on the island of Negros in the Philippines. One morning during the crusade, I awoke to find a certain pastor standing over my me bed. He had come from San Carlos City, which was almost ninety kilometers away, to find me because he had heard that I was in Jimalalud holding this crusade. He asked me to come back to San Carlos with him, so I could pray at his church for a demon-possessed young man. He told me the man was wild, violent, unpredictable, and uncontrollable, and no one knew what to do with him.

The crusade service that day wasn't scheduled to start until 3:00 or 3:30 p.m., so I figured I could get up there before lunch, pray for the young man, and still get back in time for the crusade later in the day. So, after getting dressed and eating a small breakfast, we got on the bus, went back to San Carlos and to this pastor's church, arriving around 10:00 a.m. Upon arriving, we discovered the young man, whose name was Edwin, was no longer there at the church. We were told that earlier that morning, he had had one of his violent and uncontrollable fits of rage where he had been trying to hit people, so he had to be handcuffed. The family was then called, and his mother had come and taken him to the home of his aunt and uncle until the rest of his relatives could determine what to do with him.

When we arrived at the family's house, I saw that Edwin was still handcuffed to the main center support post that held up the house. However, at least for the moment, he was coherent and in his right mind. I was told that he would have periods of time like this, where he seemed perfectly normal and fine, but then without any warning, he would change and begin to act violent and crazy, trying to hit and hurt anyone he could get his hands on.

When a demon possesses a man, he, along with any other demons that are with him, can come and go at will. A good example of this in the Bible is the madman of Gadara (see Mark 5:1–13). In that story, we see that when the legion of demons (commentators and translators point out that a Roman legion of soldiers, at full strength, numbered 6,000 men) that inhabited this man were not present, people could bind him with chains to try and control him. But when those demons came back and were in manifestation, that same man could easily tear those chains apart with his bare hands. Why would this man be subdued enough at certain times so as to allow people to bind him in chains, but at other times, be so strong and violent that he could literally rip those chains off, and terrorize the community? It's simple. The lead demon who possessed him, along with all his cohorts, would come and go. When he was gone, the man acted like he was in his right mind, but when the leader of the legion of demons, whose name was also Legion, came back, he and his friends once again took over the man's spirit, controlling his mind and his physical actions.

It's like owning your own house. You don't always have to be physically inside your house to maintain ownership and possession of the house, right? You go to work, or go off to school, or leave the house on some errand of some kind. When you do, you're no longer in your house—but it's still your house. You own it, whether you are physically present or not. This is the same truth that governs demon possession, which is why at times it may seem like a demon-possessed person is perfectly normal, but then without warning, may go off into wild fits of insanity and dangerous and unpredictable behavior.

I sat down with Edwin and my pastor friend, and we began to talk. I found him at this time to be a bright, intelligent young man. I didn't ask his age, but my guess would've been around twenty years old. I asked him if he knew he was possessed by demons, and he answered "yes" right away. He was very well-mannered and polite in all his answers to my questions. Because of this, some of his relatives asked me if it would be all right to remove the handcuffs and let him walk around. Since he appeared to be okay, I agreed, and he was turned loose while we continued to talk with him.

When I questioned him about the demons, he said there were seven demons that would come and enter into him. When I asked how he knew this, he said he could see them coming to him. He said that once the demons entered him, he was unable to remember anything that happened after that. Those were the times where he would go wild, act insane, and terrorize the family and the neighborhood. We talked together for more than an hour. He told me that these demonic attacks began when he started to hang around the Jehovah's Witnesses. It was during his association with members of that cult that these evil spirits gained access to his spirit.

All during this interview and conversation, there had been absolutely no signs of insanity or demon possession. He looked, talked, and acted completely normal. So, because time was becoming a factor for me in getting back to Jimalalud for the afternoon crusade, I instructed both Edwin and his family about how to resist the devil when he came back. They all listened and seemed to understand. Since it was now around noon, I prepared to leave and go back to Jimalalud on the bus. Just as I was walking out the door, the demons came back.

Although I didn't see the demons myself, we could clearly see the effect they had on Edwin when they entered into him. Right in front of us, his eyes changed from soft and warm to sharp and cold. A few moments before, he had been talking with me calmly. Now he was screaming in my face, and he climbed up into a second floor window, where he started taking his pants off. He was making obscene gestures with his hands and body, and as he looked down at us from the window, he kept shouting, "In the name of Jehovah! In the name of Jehovah! In the name of Jehovah!" It was obvious the evil spirits possessing him had come from the Jehovah's Witnesses cult, exactly as Edwin had said earlier in our conversation.

I told the four or five men who were present to get him down out of the window and put the handcuffs back on him. But now because he was under such demonic influence and control, he was much stronger than before, and much stronger than a normal young man his age. So it took these men a great deal of time and effort to pull him out of the window, wrestle him to the floor, and put the handcuffs back on. As they were attempting to tie his feet with rope, he managed to kick one of the men hard in the knee.

With his hands now handcuffed and his feet bound with rope, the young man could not walk or stand up. So, I had the men lift him up and stand him on his feet. One of the pastors who had been there when we got to the house started walking around Edwin, praying with his eyes closed and his head down. As he did this, Edwin kept trying to reach out and bite the man. Now up to this point, I had been sitting in a small wooden chair on the other side of the room, telling my companions and family members what to do, and waiting upon God for further instructions. But when the young man tried to bite the pastor who was walking around him in prayer, the Spirit of God rose up in me with great indignation.

I jumped out of that chair and in three steps was across the room and had Edwin by the front of his shirt. Before I realized what I was doing, I picked him up off the floor, threw him over my shoulder, and slammed him back down onto the floor. The whole house shook when he hit the floor, and his mother started screaming.

Well, you can imagine that by this time, the whole neighborhood had come to see what all the commotion was about. People were jammed into every doorway or window available, watching this deliverance unfold. Once I got Edwin's screaming mother out of the room, I began to cast out the demons. With Edwin flat on his back on the floor, I sat on his chest and got my nose about three inches from his face. I also had my finger in his face, demanding the demons to come out in no uncertain terms. Every time I commanded the demons to come out in the name of Jesus, the demons, using the man's voice, would say they were not coming out in the name of Jehovah. This had gone on back and forth for about ten minutes, when all of a sudden Edwin spit in my face, hissing and growling as the demons continued to tell me they were not going to come out.

I'm not sure if it was God being angry within me or if it was my own righteous indignation, but when he spit in my face, I took the palm of my hand and slapped Edwin across the face as hard as I could. His head literally hit the floor and bounced back up, and I again commanded these demons to come out. Again he spit in my face! Again I slapped him hard across the face, and again his head hit the floor and bounced back up. This kind of violent exchange went on for several more minutes, and when I could see he was getting ready to spit in my face again, I raised a closed fist and told him if he spit in my face one more time, I would punch him so hard his teeth would come out the back. He swallowed his spit.

This titanic struggle went on for a while longer, when all of a sudden Edwin went limp on me. All of his demonic strength seemed to abate, and he kept saying, "I surrender. I surrender!" But I knew by the Holy Spirit's witness within me that the deliverance hadn't yet taken place. I knew the devil was playing games, hoping I would take the bait and cease in my efforts to cast him out. At times like this, you thank God for all those times of performing the seven priorities of life consistently, because that kind of effort produces an ability to clearly hear the Holy Spirit's voice within, and discern the situation as it really is.

As everyone in the room began to praise God and rejoice in Edwin's deliverance, I knew in my spirit the devil was bluffing. He was still in there, had not relinquished control of this man, and I knew it. We all left Edwin on the floor while I took a break and went into the kitchen to eat some lunch that had been prepared earlier while we had been interviewing Edwin. I wanted the family to take him down to the local police station so they could put him behind bars until he was completely set free. I told the family I had to leave because of the crusade service that afternoon, but that I would return the next day to continue the deliverance of Edwin. Well, his mother didn't want to send him to the jail, so I then suggested that he be handcuffed again to the main support beam in the house until my return. This his mother agreed to do.

The reason Edwin had to be either locked up or tied up was because demon-possessed people are unpredictable and very dangerous. You can't let this kind of demon-possessed person walk around freely, either in your house or out in the public. This kind of crazy man can easily go berserk and hurt, harm, or even kill people, so you can't take any chances with him until you know he's truly free.

I went back to Jimalalud and conducted the afternoon crusade as scheduled, where I preached salvation and prayed for the sick. The next morning, as promised, I returned to San Carlos city and went back to Edwin's house to continue the deliverance. As we prayed and took authority over those demons that day, Edwin was finally delivered and set free. The last report I heard about him some months later was that he was still walking in freedom, had been saved, and was now preparing to enroll in Bible school. Praise God for that.

We must all be strong to deal with demons like the ones that inhabited Edwin. That's why you must use your time wisely every day. You never know when the next surprise attack will be—against you, your family, or your ministry. You never know when you will be called upon to draw upon your spiritual reserves of strength, so be alert and stay ready. Be consistent with those seven priorities of life.

Jesus was time-conscious

If you study the life of Jesus, you will find that He was a very time-conscious individual. He told His disciples not to labor for the meat that perishes, but to labor for the meat that endures to everlasting life (see John 6:27). In other words, Jesus was telling us to invest our time in things that will provide us with the strength we need to successfully fight our way through this life. Jesus knew the value of time management. He also knew His enemy was not bound by time. He knew He had to make the most of His time if He was to defeat the devil. He was consistent with the seven priorities of life daily, and that's why He was so strong in spirit—the strongest spiritual man that ever lived on earth. Jesus was always talking about things in relation to time. Here are a few examples:

John 2:4

4 Jesus said to her, "Woman, what does your concern have to do with Me? My hour has not yet come."

John 12:27–28

27 "Now My soul is troubled, and what shall I say? 'Father, save Me from this hour'? But for this purpose I came to this hour.

28 Father, glorify Your name."

John 12:23

23 But Jesus answered them, saying, "The hour has come that the Son of Man should be glorified."

John 11:9–10

9 Jesus answered, "Are there not twelve hours in the day? If anyone walks in the day, he does not stumble, because he sees the light of this world."

John 9:4

4 I must work the works of Him who sent Me while it is day; the night is coming when no one can work.

John 7:6

6 Then Jesus said to them, "My time has not yet come, but your time is always ready."

These scripture passages are all direct quotes from the Lord Himself, and there are many more in the Bible. We will be judged as to how we used or misused our time while living on earth. What will you say to the Lord when you stand before Him on judgment day? When He takes a look at each day you lived and analyzes your time management during each day, how will you fare? When He asks you for an explanation for how you managed your time daily, what kind of answer will you give Him? Think about it! Judgment day is not going to be a very pleasant experience for many Christians. The most sobering question of all to ask yourself: *How many people have died and gone to hell forever because the body of Christ in general was too entangled in the affairs of this life?* How many Christians wasted how many opportunities to witness and win souls, simply because they were too entangled with the affairs of this life to talk to people about the saving love of Jesus Christ? Read Ezekiel chapters 3 and 33 carefully. We have been given grave responsibility, my friend. As Christians, our number one job each day is performing those seven priorities of life so we stay sharp, strong, and ready to witness for Jesus any time, anywhere.

Protect your time

Have you ever taken a good look at the magazine racks at your local bookstore, drugstore, or supermarket? These stores usually have long rows of magazines, about four tiers high and nine miles long it seems. Not only are they kept in the magazine aisle, but they're also crammed up front at the checkout line as well. One day the Lord had me go down to the local supermarket and look at their magazine aisle. As I looked at all that was before me, the Lord asked me a question. He said, "Do you know why all of this is up here?" Before I could answer no, he told me why. "All of this is up here for one reason, and one reason alone—to take your time away from Me." In a moment, I saw it. I saw exactly what the Bible was talking about when it tells us not to be entangled in the affairs of this life.

Look at the magazines in your supermarket, drugstore, or bookstore, and note what you see. You'll find every kind of magazine imaginable, highlighting every kind of subject conceivable. For those who follow the news, there are a half dozen news magazines from which to choose. If you like sports, there are magazines that cover every possible sport on earth. If you like gossip, they've got plenty of magazines to satisfy your cravings. Are you into you? No problem! We've got *Us, We, Them, You, Me,* and *She.*

What difference does any of that have to do with eternity, life and death, heaven and hell? Nothing at all, yet we saturate ourselves with this kind of input consistently. Of course, once again, remember that most of what you'd find on the typical magazine rack in your typical supermarket or bookstore isn't sinful per se, but it's definitely a weight. It's okay to root for your favorite sports team, but how many Christians put this sort of thing before God? I was born and raised in Cleveland, Ohio, so I have an affinity for sports teams that come from Cleveland (pray for me—I've had nothing to cheer about my entire life!), but I can't let my affection for the baseball Indians, the football Browns, or the basketball Cavaliers usurp God's rightful place of prominence in my life, and neither can you if you follow sports to any meaningful degree.

I've known Christians who would skip Sunday service without a second thought if they had the choice of going to the "big game" or missing Sunday church service. This is wrong. Do you think anyone in hell cares about who will win this year's Super Bowl? In the endless ages of eternity to come, will anyone remember, or care, who won last year's baseball World Series? Think about it.

If you like to work around the house, there are plenty of magazines just for you. You can learn how to have a *Better Home & Garden.* You can learn how to "do it yourself" when it comes to home improvement or home repair.

If you like photography, you can learn everything there is to know about how to photograph your dog, cat, sister, or brother while under a full moon on a windy night. Astronomy, model airplanes, glamour, fashion, personal hygiene, financial planning, investing, automotive, flying—each topic has its own crop of magazines to buy and read.

If you're into cars and the automotive world, you can learn how to become a "piston-head" like Big Daddy Donny Dragster, and drive a quarter mile in under five seconds, or whatever. You can learn how to jack up the rear end of your car so you're always driving downhill, or lower your car so close to the ground the worms are nervous. You can learn how to drive your car to Milwaukee in third gear. Whatever you want or need or desire in terms of cars and automotives, there's a magazine for you.

Personal hygiene? We've got you covered! No hair, but want hair? Ten magazines tell you how to make it happen. How to cut your hair, comb your hair, highlight your hair, spike your hair, shampoo your hair, dye your hair, ignore your hair—make you look like Moses in the Ten Commandments. Don't worry—you want it, they got it! Looking old—with wrinkles before your time? It's okay, you can buy several magazines that tell you how to stretch your skin so you look like Jackie Chan on steroids.

Let me repeat what the Lord told me about all of this. Everything you see on magazine racks nationwide exists for one purpose only—to find ways to steal your time away from Him. Let that sink in, because it's so very true. It's stealing your time, either directly or indirectly. Satan is always looking for ways to occupy your time with things that don't build up your spirit. All of these magazines are promoting activities that are part of the world's system, and Satan is the god of that system. It's all designed to go in a negative flow away from God. Most of these activities or interests are not sinful, but become weights that hinder us and hold us back from fulfilling our destiny and potential in Christ.

In the Philippines, we have to be strong in every area of our lives. We have to use our faith every day, believing God to supply our food, our water, our health, and every aspect of daily living. I've got many staff and family members who depend upon our monthly income for their salaries and living expenses. If I go down sick, it's more than just me who will suffer for it. To raise money to keep this ship moving forward, I have to constantly travel and minister God's Word in churches. Nothing is guaranteed—I have to believe God every week for a place to preach, and it's been that way since 1980.

In the Philippines, it continues. We make plans and set schedules, but most of the time we do so with no money to pay for what we're planning. We travel extensively throughout our church network nationwide, so not only do we need the money to pay for the travel, but we also have to use faith for our health. We can't afford to become bogged down with nagging physical ailments or problems. From my perspective, I believe it's our responsibility to stay strong and keep our faith out there working ahead of us. If the devil catches me during a time frame when I have been unfaithful to God's spiritual priorities, becoming pre-occupied with the affairs of life, I could be in big trouble.

Trying to preach and minister with "Montezuma's Revenge" is no fun, let me tell you from experience. These are things they don't teach you in Bible school. It may sound funny now, but I've been there more than once, and it's no laughing matter at the time. When I left the United States with a one-way airplane ticket in September, 1980, I honestly thought I was prepared for what lay ahead. But within two months, I discovered I was not nearly as strong as I had thought. Due to inconsistency with those seven priorities of life in my own life, I learned some of what I'm telling you the hard way.

Be consistent in the use of your time_____

If you want God's promised blessings in your life, you are going to have to make time each day for what's really important. To say that you don't have the time would be the same as calling God a liar. The only people who say they don't have the time are the ones who are entangled in the affairs of this life. Most Christians waste many hours every day.

For example, how much time is devoted each day to the business of feeding our bodies? Quite a bit. It seems there's a restaurant on every corner these days, and if you notice, they're usually full of people. That's why they're always building more. If we spent half as much time in the Bible as we do in the kitchen, we'd be spiritual giants. We'd look as imposing to the devil as Goliath did to King Saul and his army. My friend, in these last days, it's time for Christians to put away their bag of chips and pick up their Bible. It's time to quit living for the next meal and start to prioritize the feeding of our spirit man instead of our carnal man.

It might surprise you to find out how much time you spend on food-related activities every day. What's usually the first thing we think about after getting up in the morning? That cup of coffee and something to eat. What do most people do between noon and 1:00 p.m.? Go to lunch. What's the first thing we look forward to when coming home from work? Supper. What do we want before going to bed? A bedtime snack. How about after going to church on Sunday? Practically the whole church moves over to area restaurants and continues to fellowship. What does the host have waiting for us after our neighborhood Bible study? A dining table full of snacks, munchies, and soft drinks. How much time do we spend shopping for food, buying food, freezing food, thawing food, marinating food, frying food, boiling food, broiling food, and barbecuing our food? We slice it, dice it, spice it up, and cook it in the crock pot, stir fry it in the wok, or grill it on the backyard barbecue. Or, if we're in a hurry, we can just zap it in the microwave so we can eat it on the run.

Now, imagine how strong we'd be if we devoted the same kind of time, energy, and attention to the feeding of our spirit man. Many of us need to quit reading the cookbook and start reading the Bible. If you want to be consistent with the seven priorities of life, learn to keep everything in proper balance. If we prioritize correctly, there will be plenty of time to perform all seven of those spiritual priorities and take care of the affairs of life without becoming entangled in them.

CHAPTER SEVEN

It pays to be consistent

Psalms 1:1–5

1 Blessed is the man
Who walks not in the counsel of the ungodly,
Nor stands in the path of sinners,
Nor sits in the seat of the scornful;

2 But his delight is in the law of the Lord,
And in His law he meditates day and night.

3 He shall be like a tree
Planted by the rivers of water,
That brings forth its fruit in its season,
Whose leaf also shall not wither;
And whatever he does shall prosper.

4 The ungodly are not so,
But are like the chaff which the wind drives away.

5 Therefore the ungodly shall not stand in the judgment,
Nor sinners in the congregation of the righteous.

Since I started in full-time ministry in September, 1980, I have confronted the devil many times in the name of Jesus. I can tell you from experience that it pays to be consistent with the seven priorities of life. When you're surrounded and seemingly outnumbered by the devil and his lies, you need to be, as verse 3 says, a tree planted by the rivers of water. In other words, your roots are strong and deep, and the enemy can't uproot you no matter how hard he may try.

I know the importance of being consistent every day. I know how strong it makes me become in Christ. On the other hand, if I'm lazy and let my flesh have its way by not performing my spiritual priorities consistently, I'll notice a definite void or power vacuum in my heart and life. That's not a good thing. We need all the strength, power and anointing we can get in our fights of faith against the enemies of our soul.

Everybody is different, so I won't attempt to convince you that my daily routine is right or wrong for you. However, I can tell you that in my own life, getting right to these seven priorities as early as I can in the day is definitely better for me. If I wait and try to get into meaningful times of worship, praise, prayer, confession, meditation, study, and reading later as the day wears on, it's much harder to be fresh in spirit to share anything of any spiritual impact to others around me. So as much as possible, I purpose in my heart to spend my time with God first in the morning, and then afterwards take care of the affairs of life. No matter how busy my daily schedule may be, I can't allow those issues to take my time away from God. Without doubt, this is one of my biggest areas of self-discipline. In the natural, I want to jump out of bed and charge right into the daily schedule, like making phone calls, reading and answering email, and taking care of all those ten thousand things that demand your attention when running a ministry like this one.

As the founder and president of MKMI, I must lead my staff, provide spiritual feeding, and give spiritual guidance on both sides of the world simultaneously. When we're in the Philippines, the needs and responsibilities of the U.S. office are still there. When we're in the U.S., the needs and responsibilities of the Philippines office are still there. So, the temptation for me is to allow the work of ministry to steal my time away from God and my spiritual priorities. Each day I must overcome that temptation, and put God first. The little sign on top of my desk that says "The Top Priority is to keep the Top Priority the Top Priority" is looked at and meditated over consistently, especially when the urge to forsake my time with God for the sake of ministry work is the greatest.

Each day, I want to prioritize my time and get with God to perform the first six of those spiritual priorities. The actual time spent on each of the first six priorities will vary depending upon the leading of the Holy Spirit, but consistently doing those first six before God in my prayer closet is always the foundation for a great day in Jesus. If I maintain consistency in my time with God in doing those first six priorities, it puts me in position to go out and witness effectively during the rest of the day—which is sharing, or priority number seven.

This discipline is tested on a regular basis by the enemy and by the everyday affairs of life. It's also tested when I travel and I'm away from home in a hotel someplace for a meeting. The pull of the world is great. It's easy on the flesh to put off your spiritual responsibilities. The devil will always whisper in your ear and tell you that it's okay to skip these seven priorities today—you can just make up for it tomorrow. But have you found out like I have that in most cases, you don't make up for it tomorrow? Once you give place to your flesh, it's easier to do it again tomorrow, and the next day, and the next day, so that before you know it, weeks have passed by since your last significant time of fellowship with God. Don't let that happen to you anymore. Seek the Lord, have Him work out a practical schedule for you to follow each day, and then stick to it. If you do, you'll see the results—guaranteed. Your schedule may be different than mine and different from those of others, but if you let the Lord chart your course for your day, He'll give you the workable schedule that will bring you to the place of great spiritual strength and keep you there.

Three groups

When the Lord first gave me the list of seven priorities of life, He categorized them into three basic groups.

Group One

1. Worship
2. Praise
3. Prayer

Group Two

4. Confession
5. Meditation
6. Study and reading

Group Three

7. Sharing

The priorities in Group One help develop our relationship and fellowship with God. That is why this group ranks the highest of the three groups. Without a real and meaningful relationship with God our Father, our efforts to please Him will be in vain. The original plan of God was to create a man with whom He could have fellowship—to give Himself someone to love. Above all else, God wants our hearts to be knit together with His.

The priorities of Group One are the things we do to build a warm and vital relationship with our heavenly Father and with our Lord Jesus who is at His right hand. In worship, we recognize God for who He is. In praise, we recognize God for what He does, and in prayer, we establish an open line of communication between heaven and the heart. We must know God before we can effectively work for Him in the name of Jesus. This was one of Paul's four main goals in his life and ministry.

Philippians 3:10–11

10 that I may know Him and the power of His resurrection, and the fellowship of His sufferings, being conformed to His death,

11 if, by any means, I may attain to the resurrection from the dead.

Notice in verse 10, he says he wants to know God. Knowing God like we must can only come by spending time with Him. There is no other way. The more time we spend with God, in worship, praise, and prayer, the more we'll get to know Him and understand Him. You know, when I call Ethel on the phone, I don't need to identify myself to her when she answers. Without the benefit of caller ID or having me tell her that it's me calling, she just knows it's me because she knows my voice. We've been married since May 7, 1983, so we've been together for all these years since. We know each other very well because we've spent time together—lots of time together. So, if she calls me, I don't need to check caller ID to see who this is—I know her voice. This is the way it should be for us in knowing our heavenly Father, and it can only happen when we make time to perform the first three priorities, which is Group One.

God is our Creator—we are His creation. We must keep that fact in mind if we are going to amount to anything in this life. Great victories are won by Christians who major in worship, praise, and prayer. This is the "top of the line"—the group of priorities that establishes a firm foundation each and every day.

The priorities of Group Two help develop and educate our spirit. This group deals with the educational processes of man at work throughout the course of life. Why is this important? We can't just know God, because He is not all there is out there. We also have to know our enemies if we're to be victorious over them as we're commanded to. Performing Group One priorities will give us an intimate knowledge of our God, which is the platform and foundation for all else. Then, we take care of the Group Two priorities so that we have a real and working understanding of how God works on earth, how the enemy works against us, and how we use our authority to enforce his defeat. The Word of God tells us that God's people are destroyed for lack of knowledge (see Hosea 4:6). We increase our knowledge in these areas by confessing God's Word, meditating on the Word, and studying and reading the Word. Notice that all three of the priorities in Group Two have to do with the Word of God. Group One priorities center around the three Persons of the Trinity—becoming intimate with the Father, Son, and Holy Spirit. Group Two priorities center around the feeding of our spirits with the Word of God. God's Word is spiritual food for our human spirit (see 1 Peter 2:2 and Hebrews 5:12, 13).

Once we have taken time to establish our relationship with God, we must educate our spirit to successfully wage war against the devil and his forces. This second group of priorities represents the process of acquiring information needed to exercise authority and have dominion on this planet, as God intended from the beginning. As we consistently feed our spirits with God's Word, we become nourished and built up in the Lord. We read, study, and meditate on the Bible to build faith into our spirit man. Then we confess the Word to release that faith and put it to work for us. This group of priorities is designed to prepare us for battle against the devil, the world system, and our unregenerate flesh.

Group Three simply consists of one priority—sharing. Sharing the gospel and witnessing are one and the same thing. By first performing the other six priorities of life, you prepare yourself to go out and effectively witness and share your faith. 1 Corinthians 4:20 says that the kingdom of God is not in word, but in power. Therefore, evangelism without the anointing of God for confirming miracles, signs, and wonders is a waste of time. Priorities one through six put you in position for God to release His power through you when you witness—priority number seven. Sharing is the Great Commission in action—the doing of Mark 16:15–20.

The order is important

When the Lord gave me this list of seven spiritual priorities, He also told me they were listed in descending order of importance. They are all important obviously, but in relation to one another, priority number one is the most important, followed by priority number two, and on down to number seven.

Also, it's important to realize that even though the list of priorities is in descending order of importance, you don't have to perform all of them in that exact order every time. Let God guide and direct you in this by His Spirit. You don't have to make this into an exercise of works. Relax and let the Lord chart your course each day as you take care of these seven priorities. The important thing is to be consistent in all of them daily, no matter which ones you do first, or which ones you do last. You don't have to worship God first, then praise God, then pray, then confess the Word, then meditate, and so on. Depending upon the daily schedule that works best for you, you might start out with some Bible reading and meditation early in the morning, and spend time worshipping God later in the day. Or, you might find that worship and praise work best for you during your lunch break at work, with Bible reading and study being performed before you go to work, or after you get home from work. And of course, sharing can take place anywhere at any time, as the opportunity arises (see Galatians 6:10). You only have to understand that worship is most important of the seven, then praise, then prayer and so forth. Feel free to rearrange the performance of these seven priorities on a daily basis, as the Holy Spirit directs you.

When you are careful to consistently perform the seven priorities of life, then you will have the strength necessary for effective ministry.

Missionaries need to be strong

One time, while I was living on the island of Bohol in Tagbilaran City, we were scheduled to conduct a crusade in a small town on Mindanao. The only way to get to where we had to go was to take a boat from Bohol to Mindanao, which left from the small town of Jagna, which was three hours bus ride from Tagbilaran. So, for the first three hours of this trip, my small support team and I were stuffed like sardines into the back of an old, run-down bus, traveling over dusty, rocky roads to reach the boat pier in the town of Jagna. We then sat on the pier (not on a chair or bench at the pier, but literally on the pier) from 5:00 p.m. to midnight, waiting for the boat to arrive from the island of Leyte. It was supposed to be there around 7:00 p.m., but as usual, it was very late, so hundreds of people, including us, sat on the pier waiting until it showed up. The wind was blowing in off the ocean and it was very cold, so everybody was huddling up as best we could to stay warm until the boat arrived. Eventually, we got so tired of sitting we laid down and tried to get some sleep, not knowing when, or even if, the boat would show up. Since we had no provisions for this, we put our Bibles down on the cold concrete pier and used them for pillows. That was the best we could do to try and stay warm and get some sleep at the same time.

After midnight the boat arrived—already jammed and overloaded with people from Leyte. There were no cots available anywhere on the boat, and there was no place to even sit down. The people from the shipping lines tried to tell everyone that there was no more room for new passengers on this boat, but of course, nobody paid any attention to them. So even while the boat's crew was attempting to dismiss the crowd, people began jumping from the pier onto the boat, even before it was docked. Since this was the only boat off Bohol for the next three days, people weren't willing to go home and try again later in the week. They were willing to stand all night if necessary, to get on the boat and make the voyage across the sea to Mindanao.

My support team looked at me and asked what we should do. I said, "It's time to jump!" So along with hundreds of others, we worked our way along the edge of the pier (being careful not to either fall into the water or get pushed in from people surging behind us). We found a target landing zone on the boat, which was about ten feet away from the pier, which was still moving because they weren't going to dock the boat due to the fact it was already full and overloaded. We jumped from the pier to the boat, and thank God, everybody made it safe and sound. But of course, there was no place to go to either sit down or lay down—the ship was already completely full. Down below deck in the passenger compartments, there were people everywhere. Cots designed for one were holding three or four. People were sitting or even laying on the filthy dirty floor in between the cots. There was absolutely no ventilation down there, so the smell of body odor was terrible and overwhelming. Rather than having everyone stand on their feet all night in that sweat parlor, I decided to take my team up top again and see if we could find any place to rest there.

When we got up on deck, the situation was the same. People were everywhere. Some standing, some sitting, some laying on the cold hard deck. So, I decided to keep going up. We literally climbed up the outside hull of the ship to the roof. When we got up there, we found more people already up there, too. But praise God, we managed to find enough room to lie down on the asphalt-roof deck. We had no blankets and no warm layers of clothing, so we used our backpacks as cushions, our Bibles as pillows, and huddled together as best we could to stay warm.

Once the boat got back out into the open sea, the temperature really dropped. The wind blew strong all night, and it was very cold. We were huddled there on the roof deck freezing, with very little shelter from the wind, from about 1:00 a.m. to sunrise. In addition to the cold, the wind blew in such a way that the smoke from the ship's smokestack was going right over us all night long. So when we got to Butuan at sunrise, everybody up on the roof that night was covered in soot and ash from the smokestack. We tried to clean up as best we could, but there was no running water, no soap, no nothing. We dusted off and waited for the sun to rise and the ship to reach port.

Our boat was going to Butuan City, a large city on the northeast coast of Mindanao. However, Butuan doesn't have a deepwater seaport with continuous access to the ocean. The city is located two miles upriver from the ocean, so if the tide is high, the boat can make it all the way upriver to dock and discharge passengers and cargo. But if the tide is low, the ships can't make it up to the city's pier because the river becomes too shallow. They have to dock where the river meets the ocean, and passengers have to disembark there and make their way to the city on foot or any available commercial transportation. Of course, we got there at the bottom of low tide. So, we had to dock at the river's mouth and carry all our luggage almost one mile to the road to get to passenger jeeps and busses, which were waiting to take us into Butuan City.

By this time, we'd already been on a beat-up old bus for three hours to get to Jagna, then waited for seven hours at the pier for the boat. Then, we had leaped from the pier to the boat, endured a frigid night as we crossed the sea to Butuan, and gotten covered in soot and ash from the ship's smokestack. Now we had to walk a mile to get additional transport to the city. That's not the end of the journey either. After finally reaching the city central around 10:00 a.m., we transferred to another old, beat-up passenger jeep, and rode another twenty-five miles north to the town of Cabadbaran, where our crusade was scheduled to start that afternoon.

If you're not strong, you won't make it. By the time we got to Cabadbaran, you can imagine how dirty and exhausted we were, but hey—we were there and the crusade started in two hours. So, we sucked it up, got cleaned up as best we could, and got ready to preach. There was no hotel in this small town, so my team and I stayed with church members from the church sponsoring the crusade. The house I stayed in had no air-conditioning and no soft bed to lie down on. After all the ordeals of our trip so far to this point, my "bed" for the next four days would be a bed of wooden boards, with a small fan that blew the hot air around in my "room." If you haven't been consistent with the seven priorities of life, you'll quit and go home.

After an hour of "resting" on the wood planks, we started setting up for the opening service. The crusade was being conducted in the local bus terminal. When we began, there were about a hundred people in attendance. I made some preliminary remarks to the people, then got right into the salvation message. While I was in the middle of my message, a man appeared out of nowhere and walked right up to the front of the stage. He pointed his finger toward the sky and started shouting at the top of his voice. It was obvious to me that he had been sent there by the devil, and I discovered later that in fact it had been his intention to disrupt and destroy our meeting that day.

After all the physical hardships endured just to get to this place, the last thing you want or need is a spiritual confrontation like this. What do you do? You're exhausted physically, but the responsibility is still on your shoulders to deal with this kind of disruption. You're the leader, so people are looking to you and expecting you to lead. I had no ushers to deal with this man for me. I had no song leaders or band members to start up some music while we escort this person away. The workers who came with me from Bohol were inexperienced, immature Bible school students. The pastor who sponsored the crusade was a babe in Christ. His attending members were clueless. There were no police anywhere to be found to help me restore order. I couldn't ask someone to just take him away, because there was no one present with the authority to do that, much less the courage to even attempt it. I knew I was on my own, and that's when all the days, weeks, months, and years of consistency pay rich dividends for God's glory. It moments like this, you're sorely tempted to feel alone, but you're never alone in Jesus. He's always there, and He doesn't get tired, exhausted, short-tempered, or cranky.

2 Corinthians 12:9–10

9 And He said to me, "My grace is sufficient for you, for My strength is made perfect in weakness." Therefore most gladly I will rather boast in my infirmities, that the power of Christ may rest upon me.

10 Therefore I take pleasure in infirmities, in reproaches, in needs, in persecutions, in distresses, for Christ's sake. For when I am weak, then I am strong.

From many experiences like this one, I know what Paul meant when he said God's power is perfected in weakness. When the devil waits until you're as exhausted as possible, then openly challenges you in public, you have to have the strength to defeat him publicly. He always tries his best to wait until your level of physical strength is the lowest, because he's always looking to gain an advantage through our flesh. The people who come to a crusade like this don't know who has the real power until the one with the real power demonstrates it. If a choice has to be made, people will always choose to follow the person with the greatest power. If you haven't been consistent with the seven priorities of life, a situation like this will make you look like a fool. Tired body and all, you have to rise to the occasion and soundly defeat the devil.

Before I had time to think, I threw my Bible to one of the crusade workers and jumped off the platform. I walked right up to this disruptive man and stood toe to toe in front of him. The crowd spread out, giving us plenty of room, expecting a fight to break out at any moment. I stuck my finger in his face and commanded him to bow his knee to Jesus Christ right then and there. He shouted back in my face, and began backpedaling, but I stayed right with him and wouldn't let him get away. With my finger still right in his face, I continued to command him to bow his knee to Jesus. He then lowered his head and refused to look at me. Finally after several more commands to bow his knee in Jesus' name, he smiled a big smile and bowed down as I had been commanding him to do. Right there in the middle of the bus terminal, he bowed like an actor after a stage performance. His power had been broken in Jesus' name, and he no longer had any influence to disrupt our crusade meeting. When I saw that he wasn't going to cause any more problems, I asked some of the church members who were standing beside him to escort him away. He offered no resistance as he was led away, and that's the last we saw of him for the duration of the crusade.

I went back up onto the platform, and resumed my message. The power of God fell upon me and many were saved and healed. They had seen with their own eyes the superior power of God over that of the devil. They had seen with their own eyes that *"greater is He in us than he that's in this world"* (see 1 John 4:4). Even with a bone-tired body, there is no limit to what you can do in Christ. It isn't you doing what you're dong—it's Christ working in you to will and to do of His good pleasure (see Philippians 2:13). All He requires of us is the consistent performance of certain spiritual priorities that position us to be used the way He wants as His co-workers and co-laborers (see 2 Corinthians 6:1).

Deliverance of former satanic priest

In another place on the island of Mindanao, I talked at length with a man who was once mightily used by the devil. He was set free when a local pastor cast the devil out of him, and I got to meet him when I went to this pastor's church to preach. The pastor introduced me to this man, who by then had become a deacon in this particular church. After service one day, we sat down and began to talk about his days as a satanic high priest. He had a footlocker, which he opened to show me, revealing some of the tools and weapons Satan had given him to use. He told me the devil himself had appeared to him on three separate occasions, giving him the things he was now showing me, along with instructions on how to use them. He said that each time the devil appeared to him, it was at midnight and always in the cemetery. That sounds just like the devil, doesn't it?

He said Satan had promised him many things—even that he would become a billionaire if he stayed faithful in black magic and the works of darkness. As an example, he said the devil showed him how to make counterfeit money, giving him a metal contraption that this man was now showing me. It was old and rusty, but he assured me that when this piece of equipment was new and under the devil's "anointing," he could make excellent counterfeit money that nobody could spot or identify. He also showed me a picture of himself standing next to a strange looking machine at the back of his house. He said its purpose was to make gasoline from ordinary water. As long as he continued to do the devil's bidding, this crude-looking machine continued to make gasoline from water. He admitted he had no idea how the machine worked, but he said it worked anyhow. When he put water in one end, gasoline came out the other end. The devil had obviously put a heavy anointing on this man.

Continuing to go through his footlocker, he showed me a Catholic scapular, which is a plastic holder containing "holy" cards and religious "prayers" to be worn around the neck. I remember many Catholics when I was growing up used to wear them, since they were told by the priests that wearing this would bring everything from good fortune to protection to answered prayers. I myself wore one many times during my early years in Catholic grade school. But unlike what the Catholic priests told us about how the scapular would help us and keep us close to God, this man told me his scapular had the opposite effect. He said that when he wore it, it had the power to make him invisible—nobody would be able to see him. He was told and promised that as long as he served the devil faithfully, no one would be able to see him whenever he wore that particular scapular.

Next, he showed me an army flak belt from the World War II era. The devil told him that the belt would protect him from any kind of physical harm, as long as he continued to obey and do what he was told to do. Most of this man's involvement with the devil took place during World War II, when the Japanese occupied the Philippines. He told me that during that occupation, many Japanese soldiers had tried to kill him, but could not do so as long as he wore that flak belt. When they shot at him, the bullets would bounce off and fall at his feet. When a Japanese soldier attempted to stab him with his bayonet, an unseen force prevented the knife from penetrating his body. He said the devil's power was protecting him as long as he obeyed and did as he was told to.

Lastly, at the bottom of the footlocker, he pulled out a steel machete. It was encased in a wooden sheath and had a wooden handle. Latin words were carved into the sheath, and more words were etched onto the steel of the blade itself. While faithful to the devil, this was his instrument of death, used to kill anyone he or the devil wanted to kill. According to him, whenever he spoke those Latin words given to him by the devil himself, the machete came out of its sheath under its own power. He said he never had to touch the blade—it would come out all by itself when he spoke those particular words. He also said the blade could not be removed from its sheath by any other means—until he, and only he, spoke those Latin words. No one else could remove the machete from its sheath, for it was held in place by the power of the devil himself. But if he was told to use it, and spoke those Latin words, the machete came out of its sheath, hovered in midair until further instructions were given, and would then go forth to kill whomever was the particular target. This man told me emphatically that this blade could and would go anywhere in the world and kill upon command. Once its assignment was complete, the machete would return and re-enter its wooden sheath. The man told me he killed many Japanese soldiers with this blade during World War II. He said the victims could not see the blade coming, but could hear it slicing through the air. It would behead a man with one pass, and then return to its sheath.

When the pastor prayed for this man's deliverance in Jesus' name, the devil tried to keep him bound. He told me that when the pastor prayed for him, the devil slashed at his face like someone slashing him with a razor blade. As the man sought his freedom in Jesus, his face suddenly would split open and begin to bleed profusely, exactly the way it would if accidentally cut with a sharp razor blade. Still the pastor continued to pray for his deliverance, and eventually the man was completely set free.

This man, who had once served the devil like this, was now a deacon in his local church and holds Bible studies as an outreach extension of his local church. The pastor who was used by God to set him free is a man who has a track record of consistency with the seven priorities of life. He was nobody special—just a man of God who was used by God in the mountains of the Philippines to set this man free. There was no featured article about any of this in leading Christian magazines worldwide, and he couldn't have cared less. His ministry wasn't large, and neither was his church. They were a group of mountain farmers living off the land, living in poverty—but pastored by a man who knew who he was in Christ.

Nothing shall be impossible to you

If you think all of what this man told me is just foolishness or a figment of his wild imagination, you need to take a trip and see the world—the real world—not some five-star hotel on somebody's beach somewhere in the Caribbean. Most people in other countries don't live like Americans, and many Americans seem to have a hard time understanding that. American Christians will have to travel farther than their neighborhood Starbucks if they are ever going to find out how things are in other parts of the world—especially the remote and rugged parts of countries like the Philippines.

In places like the Philippines, Satan's power is real and can be deadly—especially in "third world" countries and tropical zones of the earth. One of my spiritual mentors, especially in the early days of my Philippine ministry, was Dr. Lester Sumrall. He not only served the Lord faithfully for decades as a man of God, but he spent a large portion of that time serving as a missionary in the Philippines. One of the most dramatic testimonies of deliverance I've ever read about came through Dr. Sumrall's hands while trying to build his church in Manila, working to deliver a woman named Clarita Villanueva.

Especially if you're skeptical about what this man had told me about his days as a servant to Satan, I'd encourage you to read Dr. Sumrall's book entitled *Run with the Vision*, where he details the incredible deliverance of this woman in front of news media, prison officials, prisoners, and dozens of prominent local city officials. If you ever go into places like the mountains or prisons of the Philippines, you'll quickly discover the truth about the power of the devil and God's power to subdue it.

Too many Christians try to rely on somebody else's faith to pull them through in times of intense attack. But God expects all of us to learn how to stand on our own two feet. You do that through hard work, diligence, determination, discipline, and consistency of action. Hebrews 4:11 tells us all to "*labor to enter into the rest of God.*" That labor is the only work the New Testament believer is responsible for—the labor of entering His rest. It's the work of faith—learning how to trust God and rest in Him. Learning how to cast "*all your cares*" upon Him, fully persuaded that He cares for you (see 1 Peter 5:7). Even though we're commanded by Jesus to love one another, as He tells us in John 13:34, 35, we can't even do that without faith. Why? Because many times we love not because we want to, but because we're commanded to. Have you automatically loved everybody who calls themselves Christian? I haven't, and neither have you—so there are plenty of times we love by faith, not by feelings. The work of faith is the true work of the New

Testament believers—learning how to labor to enter into His rest and to stay there.

Don't misunderstand me here. We need the five-fold ministry of the apostle, prophet, evangelist, pastor, and teacher, as outlined in Ephesians 4:11. But other men and women are not supposed to fight your fights of faith for you. Their job is only to help you resist the devil for yourself. True strength will never come through the ministry of others on your behalf. You can only get strong and stay strong by making the decision to get serious with God every day. You do that by performing the seven priorities of life on a consistent, daily basis.

Too many Christians think they need more "revelation," or they need to go to some meeting and have someone lay hands on them or speak a "word" over them. Too many of us place ministers up on pedestals, and ascribe to them more importance than is needed or necessary. It's time to stop all of that immature activity and come to the realization that in Christ we can do all things. We can do all things—not somebody else doing those things for us. Listen, my friend—if you want consistent victory in your life, it's up to you and it's all under your control. You don't need "Brother Big" to come visit your church and preach. You don't need Pastor Perm, Randy Radio, or Tommy Television. You don't need 217 new CD teaching sets from Bishop Big Mouth, and you don't need to watch 39 seminars with Sister Satellite. If it's a "revival" you think you need, you can create that all by yourself, in the privacy of your own prayer closet—anytime you want. You don't need Reverend Raymond R. Revival to show up and pitch his ministry tent in your backyard. You just need to be consistent with the seven priorities of life every day.

I could give so many examples and testimonies about the strength Christians obtain and protect through consistency of action. I myself have lived this message since 1978, when I was born again and began my walk with God. I know by experience this works, and if it works for me, it will certainly work for you because God is no respecter of persons. The Word of God is for everybody, all the time in every place. Be consistent with performing the seven priorities of life, and according to Jesus in Matthew 17:20, *"nothing shall be impossible to you in Christ."*

CHAPTER EIGHT

As a man is, so is his strength

When God shares important truths with us, sometimes He chooses to use a vessel you and I would never think to use. An example of this is found in the book of Judges. In Judges chapter 8, we find Gideon chasing down the remnants of the Midianite army that had come against him. In particular, he's chasing two enemy kings, Zebah and Zalmunna. Eventually he catches up to them and captures them, and as we pick up in verse 18, he's beginning to interrogate his prisoners.

Judges 8:18–21

18 And he said to Zebah and Zalmunna, "What kind of men were they whom you killed at Tabor?" So they answered, "As you are, so were they; each one resembled the son of a king."

19 Then he said, "They were my brothers, the sons of my mother. As the Lord lives, if you had let them live, I would not kill you."

20 And he said to Jether his firstborn, "Rise, kill them!" But the youth would not draw his sword; for he was afraid, because he was still a youth.

21 So Zebah and Zalmunna said, "Rise yourself, and kill us; for as a man is, so is his strength." So Gideon arose and killed Zebah and Zalmunna, and took the crescent ornaments that were on their camels' necks.

Pay special attention to what these two condemned kings told Gideon in verse 21. "As a man is, so is his strength." This is quite a proclamation of truth, especially coming forth from two prisoners of war about to be executed. As I said, sometimes God chooses to use the most unexpected of sources to reveal something as profound as this.

Notice carefully the way this truth is worded. It doesn't say that your strength defines your identity or ability. In fact, it says the opposite. Our identity and position in Christ makes us as strong as we'll ever need to be on this earth in war. But it goes one important step farther as well. This statement reveals the fact that your level of spiritual strength is proportionate to your knowledge about who you already are in Christ.

You see, it's not enough to be seated in heavenly places with Christ and in Christ as children of God. It's not enough to legally occupy that place of spiritual superiority over your enemy the devil, as described in Ephesians 1:17–23. You have to know and believe and walk in the light of these things for yourself. There are plenty of Christians all over the world who are seated in heavenly places in Christ legally, but have no working knowledge of how strong that makes them for the work of ministry on earth. As a result, they never rise to their fullest potential as soldiers in the army of the Lord.

As a man is, so is his strength. In other words, you're only as strong as your knowledge of who you are in Christ. That's what Hosea 4:6 means when it says that God's people (that's you and me) perish for a lack of knowledge. Even Gideon himself didn't know who he was until God pointed it out in Judges chapter 6.

Judges 6:11–14

11 Now the Angel of the Lord came and sat under the terebinth tree which was in Ophrah, which belonged to Joash the Abiezrite, while his son Gideon threshed wheat in the winepress, in order to hide it from the Midianites.

12 And the Angel of the Lord appeared to him, and said to him, "The Lord is with you, you mighty man of valor!"

13 Gideon said to Him, "O my lord, if the Lord is with us, why then has all this happened to us? And where are all His miracles which our fathers told us about, saying, 'Did not the Lord bring us up

from Egypt?' But now the Lord has forsaken us and delivered us into the hands of the Midianites."

14 Then the Lord turned to him and said, "Go in this might of yours, and you shall save Israel from the hand of the Midianites. Have I not sent you?"

People love to talk about the exploits of Gideon and his three hundred men, but notice what Gideon was doing when the Lord first approached him with the assignment to save Israel from the hands of the Midianites. In verse 11, it says Gideon was threshing wheat in the winepress secretly, for fear of being caught by the Midianites. In other words, he was as scared of the enemy as everybody else was. Hiding in the winepress so as to avoid detection and punishment—this is hardly the mighty man of God we've come to admire and study about, is it?

But look at how God addresses him in verse 12. *"The Lord is with you, you mighty man of valor."* Wow! That's quite a salutation, isn't it? Especially in light of the fact that the man is hiding his work so he won't be discovered by the enemy. But once again, remember that God calls those things that be not as though they were, exactly as He did with Abraham. Go back and read Genesis, and the summation in Romans chapter 4. God was calling Abraham the father of many nations—in spite of the fact his wife had been barren her whole life, and now both he and his wife were too old to conceive and give birth anyway. Here He's doing it with Gideon as well.

"The Lord is with you, you mighty man of valor." Well obviously, Gideon didn't see himself as a mighty man of valor, did he? A mighty man of valor wouldn't be hiding in the winepress for fear of the Midianites, would he? Of course not. But you see, God wanted Gideon to see himself the way God sees him, not the way he sees himself or the way others see him. As far as God was concerned, Gideon is a mighty man of valor, even if Gideon didn't know that he is. What God had to do was get Gideon to see himself for who he really was as a servant of God. Mighty. Valiant. Triumphant. Intimidating. Overpowering. Domineering. All of that plus much more.

As a man is, so is his strength. Once you realize you're a mighty man or woman of valor for God, the strength that comes with that reality becomes available to you for battle. Once Gideon found out that he was a mighty man of valor, that's when God could begin talking to him about delivering the Israelites from Midianite occupation.

Who are we in Christ?

So, through the mouths of those two condemned kings, we understand that as men are, so is their strength. What a great statement, and what a great truth. If the knowledge and awareness of our identity dictates our level of strength, we need to know who we are, don't we? Who are we—in Christ? Since it's true that as a man is, so is his strength, then who "is" we? (Pardon the incorrect English, but I did it to emphasize the question.) Jesus gives us the answer when going about the Father's business in His earthly ministry.

Luke 11:14–26

14 And He was casting out a demon, and it was mute. So it was, when the demon had gone out, that the mute spoke; and the multitudes marveled.

15 But some of them said, "He casts out demons by Beelzebub, the ruler of the demons."

16 Others, testing Him, sought from Him a sign from heaven.

17 But He, knowing their thoughts, said to them: "Every kingdom divided against itself is brought to desolation, and a house divided against a house falls.

18 If Satan also is divided against himself, how will his kingdom stand? Because you say I cast out demons by Beelzebub.

19 And if I cast out demons by Beelzebub, by whom do your sons cast them out? Therefore they will be your judges.

20 But if I cast out demons with the finger of God, surely the kingdom of God has come upon you.

21 When a strong man, fully armed, guards his own palace, his goods are in peace.

22 But when a stronger than he comes upon him and overcomes him, he takes from him all his armor in which he trusted, and divides his spoils.

23 He who is not with Me is against Me, and he who does not gather with Me scatters.

24 "When an unclean spirit goes out of a man, he goes through dry places, seeking rest; and finding none, he says, 'I will return to my house from which I came.'

25 And when he comes, he finds it swept and put in order.

26 Then he goes and takes with him seven other spirits more wicked than himself, and they enter and dwell there; and the last state of that man is worse than the first."

This passage is broken down into three distinct parts. In casting out this demon and dealing with the resultant criticism, Jesus not only sets a man free from demonic possession, but He also reveals powerful truths about who we are, who the devil is, and what we can do because of who we are against the devil. He also shows us what happens when we fail to walk in the light of who we are in Him.

Military objective #1: Set the captives free

The first segment or part to this passage is found in verses 14 through 20. This is the Great Commission in operation—setting people free, and turning them from the power of darkness to the power of God. Jesus was casting out the demon and setting a man free who could not set himself free. This is our job, our assignment, and our task on earth as ambassadors of Christ. Nothing is ever more important than this.

No matter what you are called to do for Jesus, always remember that soul-winning is the foundation for your assignment. Winning souls is always top priority for God, so anything He tells us to do will have soul-winning as its foundation. The Great Commission of Mark 16:15–18 is the top priority on earth for God, so it's going to be the cornerstone for anything He tells you or me to do in terms of ministry.

It's so easy to be led off into great projects, outreaches, and ministries that have nothing to do with God's perfect will for you. Many Christians spend their entire lives doing wonderful things in the Name of Jesus, that Jesus never told them to do in His Name. Proverbs talks about this.

Proverbs 16:32

32 He who is slow to anger is better than the mighty,
And he who rules his spirit than he who takes a city.

Proverbs 25:28

28 Whoever has no rule over his own spirit is like a city broken down, without walls.

I realize that other popular Bible translations render these two verses a bit differently, but after much study, prayer and full-time missionary and ministry experiences since 1980, I'm well persuaded the translators got it right with their rendering of these two verses. If you don't rule over your spirit, the devil will take advantage of your own zeal for the Lord and lead you away from God's perfect will for your life and ministry. This is where so many are today in their "walk" with God. They are doing many things for Him that are all good in and of themselves but were never specific assignments from God for them to accomplish. They saw a need of some kind and launched out "in the Name of Jesus" to meet that need—never taking the time to find out if it was God's plan for them or not. In short, it's the difference between God's perfect and permissive will.

Our born-again spirit has an inherent desire to please God, worship God, and serve God. That's great, but all of that zeal has to be controlled and channeled. We must always make sure our efforts are in fact part of God's perfect will for our lives, because if they aren't, we're going to experience a lot of unnecessary frustration as we try to get things done for God.

In these two verses from Proverbs, the Holy Spirit is telling us several important things about our ministry work for the Lord. First, He tells us that if we don't rule over our own spirit's zealousness, we're like a *city broken down and without walls.* That means we become disorganized and vulnerable to satanic attack. A city that's "broken down" is one that is in chaos—with no organized structure or cohesiveness. It's a city in turmoil and confusion. Their infrastructure has collapsed, and now it's every man for himself. "Without walls" simply means defenseless. If you don't rule over your own spirit, your defenses have departed, and you have no means by which you can defend yourself against enemy attack. Remember that back when these verses were first written, cities had walls as their first line of defense against enemy attack. Jericho is a good example of this. When a city wanted to erect their defense against any enemy who would seek to conquer or kill, the first thing they did was build a wall. The wall kept the enemy out. But how long would the city stand if they were attacked and had no wall as their first line of defense? Not very long. That's the point the Holy Spirit wants for us to see here.

Our number one military objective in life and ministry is soul-winning. It has to be, because it is what God sent Jesus for, and it is for why Jesus died and rose from the dead. Yes, there are many things we can do, need to do, and must do in ministry, but we can never allow our own zeal to lead us astray and take us away from God's number one priority on earth, which is evangelism. I talk of these things from experience.

Since the beginning of our missionary ministry in 1980 in the Philippines, I've had opportunities to go off and do things that were all good for God in and of themselves, but which were things that I knew were not part of God's perfect will for MKMI. In each case, I had to respectfully decline the offer or opportunity, because I knew that if I got going in the wrong direction, it would take a lot of time, effort, and money to correct that mistake. You know, being a missionary isn't an easy thing in the natural. I know all ministries have challenges of course, but you definitely have to be called and graced by God to be a real full-time missionary. Over the years, it's been tempting to look at other ministries or activities that in the natural look more promising financially and look easier in terms of productivity. But in each case, I've said "no" because I know what I'm supposed to do, where I'm supposed to do it, and the boundaries and parameters of my work as a New Testament Apostle for Jesus.

Paul understood this, and thus was able to make this statement to the Corinthians:

1 Corinthians 9:2

2 If I am not an apostle to others, yet doubtless I am to you. For you are the seal of my apostleship in the Lord.

Paul knew he wasn't an apostle to everybody, but he was to the Corinthians. In short, he knew the boundaries of his calling and his assignment, and worked to keep himself well within those parameters. In the same way, when we decide to make ourselves available to God for ministry work, we must allow Him to dictate the terms of service, not our own zealousness.

I say all of that to emphasize to you the importance of keeping soul-winning the top priority in everything you do for the Lord. If you find yourself so involved with "ministry," but are not directly involved in the business of seeing souls saved and lives turned towards Jesus, then you better step back and seek God over the current direction of your ministry, whatever that means to you.

When Jesus was casting out that demon, He was fulfilling His ministry's work, standing perfect and complete in God's perfect will. This is our responsibility as well. We want to be active and fruitful for the Lord, but we must make sure our efforts are within God's perfect will, which will always emphasize the business of winning souls and turning hearts and lives to Jesus.

Military objective #2:
Know who you are before engaging the enemy_____

The second segment of this passage is found in verses 21 through 23. After Jesus casts out the demon and has this mini-debate with His religious critics, He makes several profound statements we would be well advised to heed. He starts talking about two men—a strong man, and a stronger man—comparing them to each other in terms of strength and ability. He says that when the strong man guards his goods and possessions, everything is fine—until somebody comes along who is stronger than he is. When that happens, the stronger man takes away whatever he wants from the strong man for the simple reason being that he's stronger. He can do whatever he wants because he can. Even though the strong man is in fact strong, he's not able to resist because the other man is stronger.

Now reading these statements in the context of Jesus delivering that man from demon possession, we come to understand that in the spiritual arena of combat and warfare, Satan is described as the strong man, but the child of God is described as the stronger man. Was the demon-possessed man able to set himself free? No. Why not? Because Satan was stronger than he was—spiritually speaking—so the strong man's goods—in this case the man himself—were intact, guarded, and under "lock and key." This man was unable to find freedom because the strong man had him bound, and he wasn't strong enough to do anything about it. But what happened when the stronger man showed up? Because he was stronger, he kicked the strong man out and the man was set free. Jesus was the stronger man, and the devil was the strong man. Look who kicked out whom.

Now, with Jesus seated at God's right hand and having delegated all His earthly authority to us, we're the stronger man in Christ. This is what God talks about in Ephesians 1:17–23. In Christ, we're seated far above all principalities, powers, and rulers of the darkness of this world. Satan is now far below us in terms of power and authority. Even though he's definitely the strong man to many, the Christian has become the stronger man by virtue of the new birth, based upon our Lord's total and complete defeat of Satan through His resurrection.

You are the stronger man

You may not feel like you're the stronger man, but you are anyway. God made you to be in Christ when He was raised from the dead (see Ephesians 2:4–10). Indeed, Satan is a strong foe. Very strong. But praise God, we're stronger in Christ. What does that mean? It means we can take whatever we want from the devil whenever we want to, simply because we can. We're like the schoolyard bully, who goes around beating up all the kids who are smaller than he is. I remember that guy, because I used to spend all of recess hiding behind trees and bushes, hoping he didn't catch me and beat me up again. Praise God, now that Jesus has stripped Satan of all the authority Adam had given him, we've become the schoolyard bully to the devil. That's how he sees us now, because that's how it is.

The schoolyard bully went around tormenting everyone else because he could. You remember him, don't you? In my school, we had several kids like this—you know—kids who for whatever reason were two or three grades behind. They were in fourth grade, but really should've been in sixth or seventh grade. So of course, because they were bigger than all the other fourth graders, they could beat us up anytime they wanted and we weren't strong enough to stop them. All we could do was try to make friends with them so they wouldn't beat us up all the time.

In this spiritual warfare, we're the stronger man in Christ. You must understand this and walk in the light of it. What happened to the madman of

Gadara in Mark, chapter 5? When the demon called Legion saw Jesus, he ran to him, fell down at His feet and on behalf of all the other demons with him began pleading with the Lord.

Mark 5:1–13

1 Then they came to the other side of the sea, to the country of the Gadarenes.

2 And when He had come out of the boat, immediately there met Him out of the tombs a man with an unclean spirit,

3 who had his dwelling among the tombs; and no one could bind him, not even with chains,

4 because he had often been bound with shackles and chains. And the chains had been pulled apart by him, and the shackles broken in pieces; neither could anyone tame him.

5 And always, night and day, he was in the mountains and in the tombs, crying out and cutting himself with stones.

6 When he saw Jesus from afar, he ran and worshiped Him.

7 And he cried out with a loud voice and said, "What have I to do with You, Jesus, Son of the Most High God? I implore You by God that You do not torment me."

8 For He said to him, "Come out of the man, unclean spirit!"

9 Then He asked him, "What is your name?" And he answered, saying, "My name is Legion; for we are many."

10 Also he begged Him earnestly that He would not send them out of the country.

11 Now a large herd of swine was feeding there near the mountains.

12 So all the demons begged Him, saying, "Send us to the swine, that we may enter them."

13 And at once Jesus gave them permission. Then the unclean spirits went out and entered the swine (there were about two thousand);

and the herd ran violently down the steep place into the sea, and drowned in the sea.

If you read the story carefully, you'll see how terrified Legion was. Looking at verse 7, we see this demon literally pleading with Jesus to extend him mercy. Imagine that—a demon pleading with Jesus for favor or mercy. That to me is amazing, but it also underscores the truths I'm sharing with you about who is the stronger man in conflicts like this. He and all the other demons that had possessed this poor soul now realized they were about to be thrown out, and there was nothing they could do to stop it. Why? Because they knew they were dealing with the Son of God, who had the authority to cast them all out. They knew they had met the stronger man. Until now, their "palace" had been well protected and secure. In other words, the man had been unable to set himself free and spent his life in misery, pain, and torment in the cemetery, crying out and continually cutting himself. But as soon as Jesus showed up, everything changed. The stronger man had now come to take whatever he wanted from the strong man.

Someone who doesn't know anything about our authority in Christ will always come along about now to say that all of this happened because Jesus was the "Son of God," implying that He could do such things but we can't. That's nothing more than pure biblical ignorance in action. What did Jesus tell us in John chapter 14?

John 14:12–14

12 "Most assuredly, I say to you, he who believes in Me, the works that I do he will do also; and greater works than these he will do, because I go to My Father.

13 And whatever you ask in My name, that I will do, that the Father may be glorified in the Son.

14 If you ask anything in My name, I will do it."

Do you believe in Jesus? If you do, He's talking about you, my friend. He's talking about anyone who is a born-again child of God—male or female. He's telling us that the same authority He operated in when on earth is now the same authority we've been given to do the same things He did in ministry. That would include casting out devils, demons, and other assorted spiritual idiots.

I would love to point out that what Jesus is talking about here isn't prayer at all, but the exercise of divine authority. You'll see Him doing this throughout His public ministry, exercising His authority to heal people, raise folks from the dead, set them free from demonic possession, calm the stormy seas, and even curse fig trees and command them to die. None of that is prayer. It's all the exercising of authority, and the authority Jesus had on earth has now been transferred to us, His church. He's the Head of the body, now seated in heaven at God's right hand. We're the body, presently operating on Planet Earth in His Name. The authority possessed by the Head must be exercised by His body on earth—and that's us!

Philippians 4:13 tells us that we can do *"all things through Christ who strengthens us."* All things. Not most things, some things, or a few things. Jesus Himself told us that the works He did we could—and should—be doing, too. Why can we do all things and do the works that He did on earth? Because in Christ, we're the stronger man, and can take whatever we want for God from the strong man, who is the devil. Daniel 11:32 says that the people who know their God shall be strong and do great exploits. Well, that includes you and me, doesn't it?

If we say we know our God, then we should be doing great things in the Name of Jesus because our God commands it. The Great Commission is not a request, but a command. 1 Chronicles 28:10 reminds us that we're called and commanded to go into all the world and be co-workers with the Lord to build the kingdom of God and ultimately get rid of the kingdom of darkness. This is why God is constantly searching for qualified saints with whom He can work and use to do great and mighty things in the Name of Jesus.

2 Chronicles 16:9

9 For the eyes of the Lord run to and fro throughout the whole earth, to show Himself strong on behalf of those whose heart is loyal to Him.

Many people read this verse but don't bother seeing it in light of its context. Let's go back and read from verse 7.

2 Chronicles 16:7–9

7 And at that time Hanani the seer came to Asa king of Judah, and said to him: "Because you have relied on the king of Syria, and have not relied on the Lord your God, therefore the army of the king of Syria has escaped from your hand.

8 Were the Ethiopians and the Lubim not a huge army with very many chariots and horsemen? Yet, because you relied on the Lord, He delivered them into your hand.

9 For the eyes of the Lord run to and fro throughout the whole earth, to show Himself strong on behalf of those whose heart is loyal to Him. In this you have done foolishly; therefore from now on you shall have wars."

When you read verse 9 in context, you see it for what it really is. This is not a general statement about God looking around for people to show Himself strong to. This is God telling us that on the field of battle, in the heat of the fight, He wants to show Himself strong to His children, who as His soldiers, actively engage the enemy. In context, God is actually upset with His people for not trusting Him in battle and for looking for help elsewhere. That's why He says that He's always looking for those who, on the battlefield, are those who trust in Him to uphold them, protect them, and fight with them. This is what you're doing when you exercise your authority as a child of God.

It's not your strength on which you're relying—it's God's strength. The definition for authority is delegated power. Ephesians 6:10 tells us to be strong in the Lord and in the power of His might. We're not the stronger man because of our strength, but because of God's. That's why when you come on the scene, exercising your God-given authority, the strong man must yield to you and give up and let go of whatever it is you want or wish to take. This is what Jesus was teaching when He compared the strong man and the stronger man.

Are you a help or a hindrance?

I think the key verse in this whole passage from Luke is verse 23. If you look at the verse by itself, it doesn't seem to have any place in this passage.

It seems disjointed and disconnected from the dialogue. But since we know the Holy Spirit inspired these writings, we know there's a purpose for Jesus saying what He said in verse 23.

Luke 11:23

23 He who is not with Me is against Me, and he who does not gather with Me scatters.

What is our Lord saying—in light of the context of this passage? Don't take that statement out of context, because you won't get what He's telling us if you do. What's the context of this verse? It's the fulfillment of the Great Commission in action. Jesus is casting out a demon and setting a man free because He's the stronger man and can take whatever He wants from the strong man, who represents the devil. Up to this point, the devil, as the strong man, had this man hopelessly bound and demon possessed. But when Jesus, as the stronger man, came upon the scene, He took what He wanted from the strong man by casting out the demon and setting the man free. So then what is verse 23 doing there?

In context, here's what Jesus is telling us. In spiritual warfare, on the field of battle, as we march forward to engage the enemy and set people free in the Name of Jesus, we must be assets to the Lord and to each other, not liabilities. In short, Jesus is saying that if you're not walking and talking as the stronger man in ministry, you're of no use to Him in spiritual conflict. Not only can He not use you, but you become a spiritual detriment, a spiritual liability, a problem for Him and for the rest of us. If you're exercising your authority as the stronger man, the man God made you to be in Christ, then you're with Him. But, if you're stumbling and bumbling along like so many Christians today, letting the devil walk or even run all over them, you're against Him.

Listen. If you're not walking as the stronger man in this life, you're actually working against the Lord, rather than working for and with the Lord. Can you see that? That's what He's saying here. If you're not for Jesus, you're against Jesus, and if you're not gathering with Him, you're scattering from Him. Instead of being an asset to the kingdom of God, you've actually become a liability. Instead of being someone Jesus can use to bring forth much lasting fruit for His glory, you become just another headache that God has to tolerate. Is that how you'd like the Lord to think of you? As a liability, a problem, or an unpleasant issue all the time?

God is in the people-saving business and has ordained this work to be accomplished through His children. He doesn't sky-write the gospel for people to read, nor does He send angels to preach the gospel in this particular dispensation. In this age of grace, we're the ones God has called upon to be His messengers, emissaries, and ambassadors. If you accept this challenge and command as a child of God, you must position yourself properly, so that in the heat of the battles you fight, God can work with you, work through you, and work for you. This can't happen if you don't see yourself as the stronger man.

I don't know about you, but for me, I can't live with the thought of being a liability to the Lord in the business of evangelism. I want to be someone He can count on, someone whom He can show Himself strong to, and someone He can depend upon in the heat of the fight. I don't need to be some kind of AWOL soldier, who's fickle and unreliable. Here's how Proverbs says it:

Proverbs 25:19

19 Confidence in an unfaithful man in time of trouble
    Is like a bad tooth and a foot out of joint.

Have you ever had a bad tooth or dislocated a bone or two? They are painful and unpleasant. It's all you can think about. The pain. The discomfort. Everything you say and do is done or said in light of the pain. It's always there, and it affects everything you do. That's how an unfaithful man is to Jesus. That's how He sees the ones who don't understand that they're the stronger man on earth in Christ.

Proverbs 25:13

13 Like the cold of snow in time of harvest
    Is a faithful messenger to those who send him,
    For he refreshes the soul of his masters.

God wants us to be like this man described here—a faithful messenger, someone who blesses and refreshes the heart of Almighty God. Would that be you today? If you're not walking as the stronger man in this life, you're not there yet.

Remember what Jesus said in verse 17. Every kingdom divided against itself will fall. Every kingdom includes the kingdom of God as much as it includes the kingdom of darkness, wouldn't it? Well, you can now begin to see why the body of Christ on earth has struggled like it has for all these centuries in regards to our God-given mandate to go into all the world, preach the gospel, and lead people to Jesus. Our kingdom has been very divided and continues to be to this day.

When it comes to doctrine and theology, understand that some of this division will go on until Jesus comes. That's just a fact. No matter how much we talk about or pray for "unity," it won't happen until Jesus returns. Unity of doctrine and unity of the faith won't become a worldwide reality until Jesus comes back to finish the seven-year tribulation and starts His one-thousand-year millennium. At that time, He's going to sit us all down and show us where we were right with our theology and where we were wrong—all of us. To think otherwise is being extremely naïve and biblically ignorant, because although the Bible emphasizes the importance of following after sound doctrine, the Bible also has much to say about how to deal with false doctrine, heresy and spiritual rebellion now, in this life, and especially in the last days. If you doubt that, re-read the letters of Paul, and discover that most of his letters dealt with heresy, false doctrine, and spiritual rebellion, to one degree or another.

We can, and should, do our best to live peaceably with all men, as it tells us in Romans 12:18. But in the context of Luke 11:14–26, Jesus is not talking about the necessity for unity of doctrine and theology per se, but about how important our unity is on the field of battle, as we go forth to fulfill the Great Commission.

Ask any soldier who has served in the military and has had to engage an enemy in mortal combat. There must be an overall awareness and cohesive mindset amongst all the soldiers in the unit. This is true for the platoon, the battalion, the division, or the army as a whole. Everybody must be on the same page, so to speak. Especially under fire, you can't have some of the soldiers following orders while others are going off to do their own thing. When men's lives are on the line in combat, everybody must work together as a single unit, because many will die needlessly if they don't. Only by sticking together as one can the unit maintain their fighting form and potential against the enemy.

From day one in basic training, military recruits are taught to work together as a team, to help each other, to protect each other, and to learn how to trust another man with their lives and have him trust his with them. This is the kind of unity Jesus speaks of in Luke 11:17. He's not talking about the unity of doctrine, which is important whenever it can happen, but in context, the unity of spiritual understanding and awareness in battle. We need to understand that unless we're all walking as stronger men and woman in battle for Jesus, our efforts will be severely crippled to the proportionate degree we have in our ranks those who don't understand who they are in Christ. This is what Jesus emphasizes once again in verse 23. If you're not with Him in battle, you're actually against Him. From God's perspective, you actually become someone who does more harm than good. I don't know about you, but that's not how I want to be described by my heavenly Father.

When we go to battle for Jesus, we can do much more for him together than we can alone. That being said, we must work to find those of us out there who understand these things, embrace them, and walk in the light of them. Within the kingdom of God, there are those of us who won't stand for living with less than what we need to carry out the Great Commission or with doing less than what our Jesus has commanded us to do. When you find such believers, love them and make them your best friends—because when the order to attack is given, you'll need every one of them at your side and at your back.

Military objective #3:
Get ready for tomorrow's counter attack

The third segment to our passage from Luke 11:14–26 is found in verses 24 through 26. Segment number one was verses 14 through 20, where Jesus was busy about the Father's business, which is our business today as well—the business of setting the captives free. Segment number two was verses 21 through 23, where Jesus informs us that we're the stronger man and can take whatever we want from the strong man, who represents the devil and his demons. This segment also reveals to us the fact that if we're not frontline soldiers walking as the stronger man for the Lord, we've become a battlefield nuisance, a distraction, and a hindrance to the work of the gospel.

This third segment talks about the future—what happens after the battle has been won and the people are set free. What does Jesus say? The demons who got cast out came back, with some of their friends this time. Listen to how Jesus describes the spiritual condition of the one who gets set free but doesn't shore up his defenses against a counter attack:

Luke 11:24–26

24 "When an unclean spirit goes out of a man, he goes through dry places, seeking rest; and finding none, he says, 'I will return to my house from which I came.'

25 And when he comes, he finds it swept and put in order.

26 Then he goes and takes with him seven other spirits more wicked than himself, and they enter and dwell there; and the last state of that man is worse than the first."

Remember Jesus is still talking about the lessons to learn in setting people free in His Name. We're still in the same discussion, and He's still talking about the truths He's put forth in verses 21 to 23. If someone is set free because one of God's stronger men or women came along and threw out the strong man, they must understand that today's triumph does not guarantee lasting victory. Victories that are won must be victories that are protected—or they'll be lost in time.

Notice that when this unclean spirit gets cast out, he wanders around for a while, seeking rest but finding none. In other words, he can't find another suitable human being to possess—for whatever reason—and so he decides to return to his former possession and see if he can get back in. When he returns, according to Jesus, the demon finds his former "house" swept and put in order. Everything is where it should be, and the place looks clean and immaculate. But that's not enough to protect that house from intruders.

Once a person is set free, they must be taught how to maintain their freedom and use their own authority to prevent the enemy from coming back in. Satan will surely come back around, and people need to know this so they're prepared for him when he tries to return. Even with Jesus, after the Lord defeated him three times with the Word of God, the Bible says Satan departed *"for a season"* (see Luke 4:13 KJV). Other translations say the devil departed until an opportune time. That simply means he'll be back. You may not know exactly when he'll try to come back, but rest assured he will try, sooner or later.

When Jesus describes this man as a "house swept and put in order," He's saying that his life has been restored, and he's back to normal in the everyday sense of the word. However, there's one glaring problem. The house, or in reality, the man, is wide open to attack. It's like describing a house that is neat, clean, and in order. Furniture is where it should be, and the place has been vacuumed and dusted from top to bottom. All the clothes are neatly placed within the drawers, closets and cabinets. Kitchen is clean, and all the dishes put away. But not only is the front door unlocked, it's wide open.

What would you think if you saw something like this in your neighborhood or anybody's neighborhood? You see someone leave for work one day and leave all the doors wide open for anyone to come in. Would you have much sympathy for the man when he came home to find his house ransacked and all his possessions stolen? I wouldn't have much, how about you? You'd think the guy got what he deserved for being so stupid as to leave his house so open and unprotected against thieves and vandals. Well, that's what happens when people get saved, healed, delivered, or whatever from God and don't take the necessary steps to learn about who they are, who the devil is, and what their responsibilities are when it comes to defending that which the Lord has provided or recovered for them.

Christians need to know that once we take care of business for God and throw out the strong man, we've got the responsibility to get ready for the counter attack. If the victory pertains to something personal in our own lives, we've got to get ready for the counter attack. If the victory pertains to someone else who we were sent to in the Name of Jesus, then our job is to inform and train them to get ready for the counter attack. Either way, get ready.

If we're not prepared for the devil's counter attack, we can actually end up worse off than in the beginning, before we were set free. That's quite a sobering fact, don't you think? Jesus said that when the demon came back, found the house cleaned up but defenseless, he not only went right back in, but took with him other demons more wicked than he.

How to get ready for the enemy's counter offensive? How to walk in the light of the fact that in Christ, we're the stronger man? Perform those seven priorities of life—consistently every day. Don't take any breaks. Don't let up. Don't slack off. Stay sharp, and stay on top of things, spiritually speaking. Keep your eyes open, scanning the horizons looking for any sign of enemy activity. Do these things, and not only will you enjoy your victories in Christ, but you'll protect them as testimonies to be shared time and again for those who need to hear.

Ezra 10:4

4 Arise, for this matter is your responsibility. We also are with you. Be of good courage, and do it.

Be strong. Stay strong.

PRAYER OF SALVATION

If you've never received Jesus as Lord and Savior, you can do that right now, wherever you are – and you don't need anyone with you to do this. Even if you're by yourself, you can pray the prayer below from your heart, out loud to the Lord, and receive the free gift of eternal salvation. Jesus stands at the door to every man's heart and knocks, but only we can open the door (Revelation 3:20)! The Bible says with the heart we believe and with the mouth we confess our salvation (Romans 10:9,10). Right now therefore, lift your heart and voice to the Lord and pray this prayer:

"Dear Lord Jesus, I believe that you are the Son of God, and that you died on a cross, paid for my sins, and rose from the dead. Therefore, right now, I open the door to my heart, and chose to make you the Lord of my life. I confess You as my Lord and personal Savior, and ask you to come into my heart now. I repent of all my sins, receive my forgiveness, and accept You as the Lord and Savior of my life – for the rest of my life. From this day forward, I will live for You and You alone, my Lord Jesus. Thank you Lord, for loving me, and saving my soul. Amen.

If you prayed that simple prayer sincerely from the heart, the Lord has heard you and done exactly what you have asked. The Holy Spirit has come and re-created your spirit man on the inside, and you are now a born-again child of God (John 3:3). This is the greatest miracle anyone can ever receive, and it happened not because of what you feel or don't feel now, but because of your faith! You reached out, and chose to receive the free gift of salvation by making Jesus Lord of your life (John 1:12 and Romans 5:17). Congratulations!

Please contact me and share the good news about your decision today to make Jesus the Lord of your life. All of heaven rejoices with you and for you (Matthew 18:12-14), and I'm so very proud of you!

Reverend Mike Keyes Sr.

ABOUT THE AUTHOR

Mike Keyes grew up in Ohio and was raised in the Roman Catholic Church. In 1973, he graduated from college to become a successful advertising executive and graphic artist. On September 21, 1978, at age 26, he was born again and Spirit filled two days later. Immediately the gifts of the Spirit began working in his life. Through his local church, he began to witness on the streets, in area prisons, and anywhere he could hand out tracts.

In September, 1979, Reverend Keyes resigned his job to attend Rhema Bible Training Center in Tulsa, Oklahoma, graduating in May, 1980. In September, 1980, he traveled to the Philippines with a one-way plane ticket, arriving without knowledge of the language or customs, and with no one there to meet him. When he got off that plane to begin his ministry, he had $20 in his pocket, one foot locker containing his Bible, class notes, a few changes of clothing, and the promise of support from no one except his parents and one small church in Toledo, Ohio, totaling $250.

From those humble beginnings and through his faithfulness to the calling of God over the years, the Lord has used Reverend Keyes extensively to reach untold numbers of people in the Philippines and around the world. Always emphasizing outreach to the remote, overlooked, out-of-the-way villages and towns that no one else has gone to, at the 30 year anniversary of his ministry work in September, 2010, it is conservatively estimated that over one half million souls have been won to Christ in his nationwide crusades in the Philippines.

Mike Keyes Ministries International (MKMI) is an apostolic ministry that reaches the lost, teaches the Christians and trains the ministers. With a consistent crusade outreach, a church network of hundreds of churches, and a 2-year Bible school, Reverend Keyes and his staff, pastors, graduates and students continue to fulfill the Great Commission wherever he is instructed to go by the Holy Spirit – throughout the Philippines and around the world.

Reverend Keyes is married to a native Filipina, Ethel, and has two children.

For additional information:

◆ About Reverend Keyes and the MKMI ministry
◆ About becoming involved in prayer or financial support
◆ About participating in our annual missions tour
◆ About obtaining more copies of this book, or other books and CD teaching sets

Please contact us at

◆ Web: www.mkmi.org
◆ E-mail: ekeyes@mkmi.org

OTHER BOOKS BY
MIKE KEYES SR

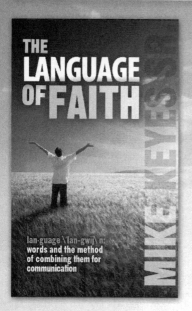

The Language of Faith
ISBN: 978-1-939570-02-4

Have you ever wondered how to communicate with God? In *The Language of Faith*, Mike Keyes, Sr. reveals the rules that govern the language of faith, how you can use those rules to speak faith, and as a result, see the windows of heaven open up on your behalf.

Divine Peace
ISBN: 978-1-939570-17-8

How can you live above fear and pressure and the frantic pace of life in these perilous times? *Divine Peace* reveals the principles of knowing and walking in God's peace every day and how to stand strong in the midst of every circumstance with a peace that passes all understanding.

OTHER BOOKS BY
MIKE KEYES SR

Helmet of Hope
ISBN: 978-1-939570-01-7

When a new recruit joins the army, he is issued a helmet and it can mean the difference between life and death in battle. Every spiritual battle is won or lost in the mind - if you lose hope, you've lost your helmet and your head is unprotected. The Helmet of Hope was written to make you a skilled soldier fully prepared for every fight of the faith.

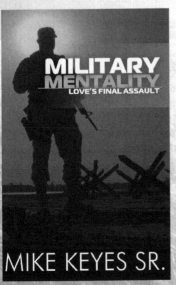

Military Mentality
ISBN: 978-1-936314-98-0

Military Mentality concerns the global war raging at this moment over the souls of humankind. The Body of Christ is at war. Our weapons are different than physical battle and our enemies are not flesh and blood. However, we can apply many crucial lessons learned in wartime to fight our fights of faith today.